Decadents, Symbolists, Anti-Decadents

Poetry of the 1890s

A series of facsimile reprints chosen and introduced by
R.K.R.THORNTON AND IAN SMALL

John Gray

Silverpoints
1893
Spiritual poems
1896

Woodstock Books
Oxford and New York
1994

This edition first published 1994 by
Woodstock Books
Spelsbury House, Spelsbury, Oxford OX7 3JR
and
Woodstock Books
387 Park Avenue South
New York, NY 10016-8810

ISBN 1 85477 144 2
Reproduced by permission
from copies in Reading University Library
New matter copyright © Woodstock Books 1994

British Library Cataloguing-in-Publication Data
A catalogue record for this book is
available from the British Library

Library of Congress Cataloging-in-Publication Data
Gray, John, 1866-1934.
  [Silverpoints]
  Silverpoints; with, Spiritual poems / John Gray.
    p. cm. – (Decadents, symbolists, anti-decadents)
  Includes bibliographical references.
  ISBN 1-85477-144-2: $48.00
I. Gray, John, 1866-1934. Spiritual poems. 1994. II. Title:
Silverpoints. III. Title: Spiritual poems. IV. Series.
PR6013.R367A6 1994   93-41357
821'.8–dc20   CIP

Printed and bound in Great Britain by
Smith Settle
Otley, West Yorkshire LS21 3JP

Introduction

John Gray's *Silverpoints* is an icon of the 1890s. It has all the hallmarks of the exquisite book, being slim and select, only forty pages long and published in an edition of two hundred and fifty copies. Its format is distinctive and elegant, only about eleven centimetres wide and twice as tall. It was bound in vellum or green cloth with a chaste design in gold by Charles Ricketts of leaf or flame shapes against a wave pattern, and it was printed at his instructions in imitation of the old Aldine books in an italic with Roman capitals at the beginning of the lines. The margins were lavish and the paper was handmade Van Gelder. The contents too declared their refinement and their place in a new movement with an epigraph '*en composant des acrostiches indolents*' from Paul Verlaine's poem 'Langueur', whose first line is '*Je suis l'Empire à la fin de la décadence*'. The dedications too, to Princess Alice of Monaco, to Verlaine, to Félix Fénéon, to Ellen Terry, to Oscar Wilde, Pierre Louÿs, Ernest Dowson, Frank Harris, read like a brief inventory of new writers and their patrons, while the fact that thirteen of twenty nine poems in the book are translations emphasises the book's new and frenchified air. Not that the translations are insignificant; Gray can be credited with introducing not only Verlaine, whom Arthur Symons had translated in *Silhouettes*, but also Baudelaire, Mallarmé and Rimbaud. The original poems are an odd mixture of eagerness to espouse the latest extremes and styles and an insistence on old and traditional values, and they share with the translations another characteristic of the book, the reticence of the author, and his habit of hiding behind an elaborate façade. The exact nature of the author himself is always concealed. Jerusha McCormack, his most recent and most convincing biographer, sees him as always creating a self behind which to hide: first 'Dorian' Gray the poet and decadent, and afterwards Canon Gray, the cool and aloof priest. The creation of the first persona and its rejection, and the subsequent search for meaning and the creation of his second persona form the story of Gray's life.

It was essential that this eldest of nine children, who lacked the advantages of a university education, *should* make himself if he were to hold his own with the aesthetic groups of the 1890s. He was born in 1866, the son of a man who was in turn merchant's clerk, wheelwright, carpenter in the Royal Naval Dockyard at Woolwich, and later inspector of stores at Woolwich Arsenal. At the age of twelve he won a scholarship to the Roan School in Greenwich, where he distinguished himself, but his father removed him after a year to apprentice him as a metal-turner at Woolwich Arsenal. At night he studied French, German and Latin and taught himself to draw, and he was promoted to the drawing office. He took competitive examinations for the Civil Service and qualified as a boy clerk for the Post Office Savings Bank in 1882, moving swiftly to the Confidential Enquiry Branch and passing a further examination in 1884 to qualify as a Lower Division Clerk. Although he registered at the University of London and passed matriculation examinations in 1887, he did not continue at university, but moved on in the Civil Service until he reached a post in the Foreign Office Library in 1893.

The centre of his interest in the late years of the 1880s was however the world of art and letters, and his most influential early contact with that world was with Charles Ricketts and Charles Shannon at the Vale in Chelsea. Ricketts took Gray under his wing and introduced him to art and connoisseurship and to the work of modern French poets. Gray's first published work was in Ricketts and Shannon's *The Dial*, an essay on the brothers Goncourt and a fairy story. Gray was encouraged to make contact with Félix Fénéon in France, who introduced him to writers and painters in Paris.

In 1889 Gray decided to join the Catholic Church, which he did formally in 1890, though the subsequent two or three years saw him behaving almost in deliberate defiance of his declared faith. In these years he associated with Wilde, whom he had first met in 1889, with homosexual writers and with avant-garde poets and artists of the time; he went to meetings of the Rhymers' Club and was involved in J. T. Grein's Independent Theatre, all the time trying to create or find his own role. He translated Théodore de Banville's *Le baiser* for performance at the Independent Theatre in March 1892. Gray was obviously attracted to Wilde as well as repelled by him, and Wilde was influential in Gray's development as a man of letters. Whether Wilde modelled some aspects of Dorian Gray on John Gray is impossible to decide, but Gray signed himself 'Dorian' in at least one letter to Wilde. Wilde even signed a contract to pay for the making and advertising of *Silverpoints*, although this was replaced by a new contract whereby the publisher engaged to bring the book out at his own expense. After a lecture in February 1892 on 'The Modern Actor', given at the occasion when Wilde chaired a discussion at the Playgoers' Club, the press began to associate John Gray publicly with Dorian Gray, and he initiated a legal action against *The Star* which brought him an apology for such association. But the moral climate was getting too hot, and in late 1892 he suffered some sort of breakdown, coming near to madness. It is in this period that his allegiance shifts from Oscar Wilde to André Raffalovich and his religious poetry begins.

Gray had met Raffalovich in 1892 and the meeting was of central importance for his later years. Raffalovich, two years older than Gray, of independent means, a Jew and overtly homosexual, took the place of Wilde, and the growing friendship helped Gray to repudiate the decadent self he had assumed. *Silverpoints* was published in March 1893 and greeted as the most decadent of productions, but within a fortnight of its publication Gray had broken with Wilde and, even though there were less than three hundred copies printed, had begun his repudiation of the book and all it stood for; in later years he made attempts to buy up copies and 'immobilise' them. Gray had begun to see his decadent phase as a part of a spiritual progression and he began to move towards the creation of his new role as Father Gray. Meanwhile he collaborated with Raffalovich on plays. His *Sour grapes* (in rhymed couplets) was one of a pair of one-act plays privately performed in 1894, and in the same year a melodrama called *The blackmailers* written in collaboration with Raffalovich was publicly performed without success at the Prince of Wales's Theatre. In 1895 Gray and Raffalovich published two duologues called *A northern aspect* and *The ambush of young days*.

From 1894 Gray began to send his friends the *Blue calendars* that emphasise his new direction. During the trials of Oscar Wilde, fearing association with Wilde, he had engaged counsel to hold a watching brief to make sure that he was not implicated, and the verdict marked a point of clarification in Gray's moral position. In 1896 he gathered together the eleven poems and twenty nine translations that form *Spiritual poems: chiefly done out of several languages*. The sources were Latin, Spanish, German and French, usually medieval and mystical. In this period he also edited a number of collections of poems and made other translations. He edited *Fifty songs* by Thomas Campion in 1896, Michael Drayton's *Nymphidia and The muses Elizium* in 1896, *Poems and songs* by Sir John Suckling in 1896, *Poems and sonnets* by Henry Constable in 1897, and *Sonnets* by Sir Philip Sidney in 1898. In 1897 he translated Nietzsche's poems, and his association with Dr Alexander Tille of the Glasgow Goethe society led to a translation in 1898 of Goethe's *Satyros and Prometheus*.

The movement towards a complete commitment to his religion was becoming more compelling. In 1896 Raffalovich became a Catholic. Gray became involved in the welfare both spiritual and physical of the dying Aubrey Beardsley, whose deathbed conversion may have precipitated Gray's decision to enter the priesthood. Some accuse Gray and Raffalovich of bribing Beardsley into the church, but Beardsley's suffering and decisions may more convincingly be seen as a spur to Gray himself. He resigned from the Foreign Office library in November 1897 and Beardsley died in March 1898. In October 1898 Gray entered the Scots College in Rome and he was ordained in 1901. He edited Beardsley's letters to Raffalovich and himself in 1904.

His first job as a priest was in the slums of Edinburgh, but in 1906-7 he and Raffalovich built a new Catholic church of St Peter's in the refined Morningside district of Edinburgh, where Gray was to be parish priest until his death in 1934, and where Raffalovich ministered over a salon which played host to Edinburgh and visiting notables.

As with Beardsley, Gray saw another passage through suffering to religious conviction in Katharine Bradley and Edith Cooper, the aunt and niece who wrote as 'Michael Field', to whom he became close in 1906. Their relationship mirrored that of Gray and Raffalovich (and that of Ricketts and Shannon), and Gray found in Bradley another image of his own struggle to discipline a too sensuous nature. He was a source of great comfort to her at the time of Cooper's death from cancer in 1913 and in her own fatal illness (with the same disease) some months later in 1914.

Perhaps feeling that literature had only been his means to a religious end, Gray published little in the new century until 1921, when he began to publish essays in *Blackfriars*. *Vivis*, of which only seventy five copies were printed in 1921, retained the sense of the esoteric in its cryptic quatrains, while *The long road* (1926), which republished most of them, extends the precise economy of a haiku into a poem of spiritual journeying. *Poems* (1931) indicates that Gray could find a voice which recognised its ancestry and yet was still modern. But the most striking book of his later years was *Park: a fantastic story* (1932), a novel whose mysterious meaning is best guessed at from a biographical perspective, seeing it as once more struggling with the problem of identity, the problem that beset Gray all his life. Raffalovich died in February 1934. Gray died in June of the same year.

In spite of some recognition of his twentieth-century work and the curiosity inspired by his novel, it is the Gray of the 1890s that most fascinates. His attempts to create a decadent but self-consciously restrained persona in *Silverpoints* and his search for a redemptive religion in *Spiritual poems* sum up the dilemma of the 1890s.

I.S.
R.K.R.T.

Select Bibliography

A saint and others: from the French of Paul Bourget, 1892.
Ecstasy: a study of happiness (translation from Louis Couperus with A. Teixeira de Mattos), 1892.
The kiss (translated from de Banville), performed 1892, published Edinburgh, 1983.
Silverpoints, 1893.
The blue calendar 1895. A book of carols, privately printed, 1894.
The blue calendar 1896. Twelve sundry carols, privately printed, 1895.
A northern aspect. The ambush of young days. Two duologues (with André Raffalovich), privately printed, 1895.
The blue calendar 1897, privately printed, 1896.
Spiritual poems, chiefly done out of several languages, 1896.
Poems (translated from Friedrich Nietzsche) in volume 10 of *Collected works* of Nietzsche, edited by Alexander Tille, New York, 1897; reprinted as volume 1, 1899.
The fourth and last blue almanack 1898, privately printed, 1897.
Satyros and Prometheus (translated from Goethe), Glasgow, 1898.
Fourteen scenes in the life of the Blessed Virgin Mary, privately printed, 1903; reprinted as *Ad matrem: poems by John Gray*, 1904; and as *Ad matrem*, 1906.
Last letters of Aubrey Beardsley (ed. and introduced), 1904.
Verses for tableaux vivants, privately printed, 1905.
Vivis, Ditchling, Sussex, 1922.
On hymn writing, Kensington, 1925.
Saint Peter's, Edinburgh: a brief description of the church and its contents, Oxford, 1925.
Saint Peter's hymns, Kensington, 1925.
The long road, Oxford, 1926.
Sound: a poem, 1926.
O beata trinitas: the prayers of St. Gertrude and St. Mechtilde (translation), 1927; reprinted as *The true prayers of St. Gertrude and St. Mechtilde*, 1928 and 1936.
The child's daily missal (translated from compilation by Dom Gaspar Lefebvre and Elisabeth van Elewyck), Lophem

near Bruges, 1930.
Poems (1931), 1931.
Park: a fantastic story, 1932; reprinted with introduction by
    Bernard Bergonzi, Aylesford, Kent, 1966; reprinted with
    afterword by Philip Healy, Manchester, 1984.
A phial, Edinburgh, 1954.
The person in question (short story), Buenos Aires, 1958.
John Gray: five fugitive poems, ed. Ian Fletcher, 1983.
The Poems of John Gray, ed. Ian Fletcher, Greensboro, N.C.,
    1988.

Further reading

Two friends: John Gray and André Raffalovich, ed. Brocard
    Sewell, Aylesford, Kent, 1963.
Brocard Sewell, *Footnote to the nineties: a memoir of John Gray
    and André Raffalovich*, 1968.
G. A. Cevasco, *John Gray*, Boston, 1982.
Brocard Sewell, *In the Dorian mode: a life of John Gray, 1866-
    1934*, Padstow, Cornwall, 1983.
*A friendship of the nineties: letters between John Gray and Pierre
    Louÿs*, ed. Allan Walter Campbell, Edinburgh, 1984.
G. A. Cevasco, *Three decadent poets, Ernest Dowson, John Gray,
    and Lionel Johnson: an annotated bibliography*, 1990.
Jerusha Hull McCormack, *John Gray: poet, dandy, and priest*,
    Hanover, NH, 1991.

Publisher's note

The exceptionally narrow format of the original *Silverpoints*
is represented in this edition by the rule in the inner margin.

SILVERPOINTS
BY
JOHN GRAY

LONDON . M.DCCC.XC.III
ELKIN MATHEWS AND
JOHN LANE . AT THE
SIGN OF THE BODLEY
HEAD IN VIGO STREET

OF THIS BOOK THERE HAVE BEEN
PRINTED...250.. COPIES . THIS IS
NO......81

ALL RIGHTS RESERVED

...EN COMPOSANT DES ACROSTICHES INDOLENTS
                                    P.V.

LES DEMOISELLES DE SAUVE

TO S. A. S. ALICE, PRINCESSE DE MONACO

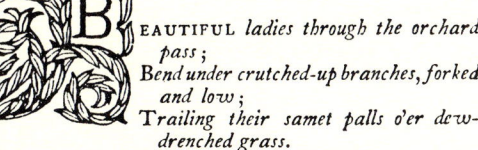

BEAUTIFUL *ladies through the orchard
 pass ;
Bend under crutched-up branches, forked
 and low ;
Trailing their samet palls o'er dew-
 drenched grass.*

*Pale blossoms, looking on proud Jacqueline,
Blush to the colour of her finger tips,
And rosy knuckles, laced with yellow lace.*

*High-crested Berthe discerns, with slant, clinched eyes,
Amid the leaves pink faces of the skies ;
She locks her plaintive hands Sainte-Margot-wise.*

*Ysabeau follows last, with languorous pace ;
Presses, voluptuous, to her bursting lips,
With backward stoop, a bunch of eglantine.*

*Courtly ladies through the orchard pass ;
Bow low, as in lords' halls ; and springtime grass
Tangles a snare to catch the tapering toe.*

HEART'S DEMESNE

TO PAUL VERLAINE

LISTEN, *bright lady, thy deep Pansie eyes
Made never answer when my eyes did pray,
Than with those quaintest looks of blank surprise.*

*But my lovelonging has devised a way
To mock thy living image, from thy hair
To thy rose toes; and keep thee by alway.*

*My garden's face is oh! so maidly fair,
With limbs all tapering and with hues all fresh;
Thine are the beauties all that flourish there.*

*Amaranth, fadeless, tells me of thy flesh.
Briarrose knows thy cheek, the Pink thy pout.
Bunched kisses dangle from the Woodbine mesh.*

*I love to loll, when Daisy stars peep out,
And hear the music of my garden dell,
Hollyhock's laughter and the Sunflower's shout.*

And many whisper things I dare not tell.

SONG OF THE SEEDLING

TO ARTHUR SEWELL BUTT

T ELL, *little seedling, murmuring germ,*
Why are you joyful? What do you sing?
Have you no fear of that crawling thing,
Him that has so many legs? and the worm?

R AIN *drops patter above my head—*
  Drip, drip, drip.
To moisten the mould where my roots are fed—
  Sip, sip, sip.
No thought have I of the legged thing,
  Of the worm no fear,
  When the goal is so near;
Every moment my life has run,
The livelong day I've not ceased to sing:
  I must reach the sun, the sun.

LADY EVELYN

I know no Name too sweet to tell of her,
For Love's sweet Sake and Domination.
She hath me all; her Spell hath Power to stir
My Heart to every Lust, and spur me on.
Love saith: 'tis even thus: her Will no Thrall,
But Touchstone of thy Worth in Love's Armure;
They only conquer in Love's Lists that fall,
And Wounds renewed for Wounds are captain Cure.
He doubly is inslaved that gilts his Chain,
Saith Reason, chaffering for his Empire gone,
Bestir, and root the Canker that hath ta'en
Thy Breast for Bed, and feeds thy Heart upon.

I this: Sweet Love, an sweet an sour thou be,
I know no Name too sweet to tell of thee.

COMPLAINT

TO FELIX FÉNÉON

M EN, *women, call thee so or so;*
 I do not know.
 Thou hast no name
For me, but in my heart a flame

Burns tireless, neath a silver vine.
 And round entwine
 Its purple girth
All things of fragrance and of worth.

Thou shout! thou burst of light! thou throb
 Of pain! thou sob!
 Thou like a bar
Of some sonata, heard from far

Through blue-hue'd veils! When in these wise,
 To my soul's eyes,
 Thy shape appears,
My aching hands are full of tears.

A HALTING SONNET

TO MISS ELLEN TERRY ON HER BIRTHDAY.

It is not meet for one like me to praise
A lady, princess, goddess, artist such;
For great ones crane their foreheads to her touch,
To change their splendours into crowns of bays.
But poets never rhyme as they are bid;
Nor never see their fit goal; but aspire,
With straining eyes, to some far silvern spire;
Flowers among, sing to the gods cloud-hid.
One of these, onetime, opened velvet eyes
Upon the world—the years recall the day;
Those lights still shine, conscious of power alway,
But flattering men with feigned looks of surprise.

> *The couplet is so great that, where thou art,*
> *—Thou being a poem—it is past my art.*

WINGS IN THE DARK

TO ROBERT HARBOROUGH SHERARD

Forth *into the warm darkness faring wide—*
More silent momently the silent quay—
Towards where the ranks of boats rock to the tide,
Muffling their plaintive gurgling jealously.

With gentle nodding of her gracious snout,
One greets her master till he step aboard;
She flaps her wings, impatient to get out;
She runs to plunder, straining every cord,

Full-winged and stealthy like a bird of prey,
All tense the muscles of her seemly flanks;
She, the coy creature that the idle day
Sees idly riding in the idle ranks.

Backward and forth, over the chosen ground,
Like a young horse, she drags the heavy trawl,
Tireless; or speeds her rapturous course unbound,
And passing fishers through the darkness call

Deep greeting, in the jargon of the sea.
Haul upon haul, flounders and soles and dabs,
And phosphorescent animalculæ,
Sand, seadrift, weeds, thousands of worthless crabs.

Low on the mud the darkling fishes grope,
Cautious to stir, staring with jewel eyes;
Dogs of the sea, the savage congers mope,
Winding their sulky march Meander-wise.

Suddenly all is light and life and flight,
Upon the sandy bottom, agate strewn.
The fishers mumble, waiting till the night
Urge on the clouds, and cover up the moon.

THE BARBER

I   I DREAMED *I was a barber; and there went
Beneath my hand, oh! manes extravagant.
Beneath my trembling fingers, many a mask
Of many a pleasant girl. It was my task
To gild their hair, carefully, strand by strand;
To paint their eyebrows with a timid hand;
To draw a bodkin, from a vase of kohl,
Through the closed lashes; pencils from a bowl
Of sepia to paint them underneath;
To blow upon their eyes with a soft breath.
They lay them back and watched the leaping bands.*

II *The dream grew vague. I moulded with my hands
The mobile breasts, the valley; and the waist
I touched; and pigments reverently placed
Upon their thighs in sapient spots and stains,
Beryls and crysolites and diaphanes,
And gems whose hot harsh names are never said.
I was a masseur; and my fingers bled
With wonder as I touched their awful limbs.*

III *Suddenly, in the marble trough, there seems
O, last of my pale mistresses, Sweetness!
A twylipped scarlet pansie. My caress
Tinges thy steelgray eyes to violet.
Adown thy body skips the pit-a-pat
Of treatment once heard in a hospital
For plagues that fascinate, but half appal.*

IV *So, at the sound, the blood of me stood cold.
Thy chaste hair ripened into sullen gold.
The throat, the shoulders, swelled and were uncouth.
The breasts rose up and offered each a mouth.
And on the belly pallid blushes crept,
That maddened me, until I laughed and wept.*

MISHKA

TO HENRI TEIXEIRA DE MATTOS

Mishka *is poet among the beasts.*
When roots are rotten, and rivers weep,
The bear is at play in the land of sleep.
Though his head be heavy between his fists.
The bear is poet among the beasts.

THE DREAM:

Wide *and large are the monster's eyes,*
Nought saying, save one word alone:
Mishka! Mishka, as turned to stone,
Hears no word else, nor in anywise
Can see aught save the monster's eyes.

Honey is under the monster's lips;
And Mishka follows into her lair,
Dragged in the net of her yellow hair,
Knowing all things when honey drips
On his tongue like rain, the song of the hips

Of the honey-child, and of each twin mound.
Mishka! there screamed a far bird-note,
Deep in the sky, when round his throat
The triple coil of her hair she wound.
And stroked his limbs with a humming sound.

Mishka is white like a hunter's son;
For he knows no more of the ancient south
When the honey-child's lips are on his mouth,
When all her kisses are joined in one,
And his body is bathed in grass and sun.

The shadows lie mauven beneath the trees,
And purple stains, where the finches pass,
Leap in the stalks of the deep, rank grass.
Flutter of wing, and the buzz of bees,
Deepen the silence, and sweeten ease.

The honey-child is an olive tree,
The voice of birds and the voice of flowers,
Each of them all and all the hours,
The honey-child is a wingèd bee,
Her touch is a perfume, a melody.

SUMMER PAST

TO OSCAR WILDE

THERE was the summer. There
   Warm hours of leaf-lipped song,
   And dripping amber sweat.
     O sweet to see
The great trees condescend to cast a pearl
Down to the myrtles; and the proud leaves curl
    In ecstasy.

   Fruit of a quest, despair.
   Smart of a sullen wrong.
   Where may they hide them yet?
     One hour, yet one,
To find the mossgod lurking in his nest,
To see the naiads' floating hair, caressed
    By fragrant sun-

   Beams. Softly lulled the eves
   The song-tired birds to sleep,
   That other things might tell
     Their secrecies.
The beetle humming neath the fallen leaves.
Deep in what hollow do the stern gods keep
Their bitter silence? By what listening well
    Where holy trees,

Song-set, unfurl eternally the sheen
    Of restless green?

THE VINES
TO ANDRÉ CHEVRILLON

"*Have you seen the listening snake?*"
Bramble clutches for his bride,
Lately she was by his side,
Woodbine, with her gummy hands.

In the ground the mottled snake
Listens for the dawn of day;
Listens, listening death away,
Till the day burst winter's bands.

Painted ivy is asleep,
Stretched upon the bank, all torn,
Sinewy though she be; love-lorn
Convolvuluses cease to creep.

Bramble clutches for his bride,
Woodbine, with her gummy hands,
All his horny claws expands;
She has withered in his grasp.

"*Till the day dawn, till the tide*
Of the winter's afternoon."
"*Who tells dawning?*"—"*Listen, soon.*"
Half-born tendrils, grasping, gasp.

Je pleure dans les coins; je n'ai plus goût à rien;
Oh! j'ai tant pleuré, Dimanche, en mon paroissien!

JULES LAFORGUE

D<small>ID</small> we not, Darling, you and I,
Walk on the earth like other men?
Did we not walk and wonder why
They spat upon us so. And then

We lay us down among fresh earth,
Sweet flowers breaking overhead,
Sore needed rest for our frail girth,
For our frail hearts; a well-sought bed.

So Spring came, and spread daffodils;
Summer, and fluffy bees sang on;
The fluffy bee knows us, and fills
His house with sweet to think upon.

Deep in the dear dust, Dear, we dream.
Our melancholy is a thing
At last our own; and none esteem
How our black lips are blackening.

And none note how our poor eyes fall,
Nor how our cheeks are sunk and sere...
Dear, when you waken, will you call?...
Alas! we are not very near.

Ainsi, elle viendrait à moi! les yeux bien fous!
Et elle me suivrait avec cet air partout!

TO E. M. G.

LEAN *back, and press the pillow deep,*
Heart's dear demesne, dear Daintiness;
Close your tired eyes, but not to sleep....
How very pale your pallor is!

You smile, your cheek's voluptuous line
Melts in your dimple's saucy cave.
Your hairbraids seem a wilful vine,
Scorning to imitate a wave.

Your voice is tenebrous, as if
An angel mocked a blackbird's pipe.
You are my magic orchard feoff,
Where bud and fruit are always ripe.

O apple garden! all the days
Are fain to crown the darling year.
Ephemeral bells and garland bays,
Shy blade and lusty, bursting ear.

In every kiss I call you mine,
Tell me, my dear, how pure, how brave
Our child will be! what velvet eyne,
What bonny hair our child will have!

CROCUSES IN GRASS

TO CHARLES HAZELWOOD SHANNON

Purple *and white the crocus flowers,*
   And yellow, spread upon
   The sober lawn; the hours
Are not more idle in the sun.

Perhaps one droops a prettier head,
   And one would say: Sweet Queen,
   Your lips are white and red,
And round you lies the grass most green.

And she, perhaps, for whom is fain
   The other, will not heed;
   Or, that he may complain,
Babbles, for dalliaunce, with a weed.

And he dissimulates despair,
   And anger, and suprise;
   The while white daisies stare
—And stir not—with their yellow eyes.

POEM

TO ARTHUR EDMONDS

Geranium, *houseleek, laid in oblong beds
On the trim grass. The daisies' leprous stain
Is fresh. Each night the daisies burst again,
Though every day the gardener crops their heads.*

*A wistful child, in foul unwholesome shreds,
Recalls some legend of a daisy chain
That makes a pretty necklace. She would fain
Make one, and wear it, if she had some threads.*

*Sun, leprous flowers, foul child. The asphalt burns.
The garrulous sparrows perch on metal Burns.
Sing! Sing! they say, and flutter with their wings.
He does not sing, he only wonders why
He is sitting there. The sparrows sing. And I
Yield to the strait allure of simple things.*

ON A PICTURE

TO PIERRE LOUŸS

Not pale, as one in sleep or holier death,
Nor illcontent the lady seems, nor loth
To lie in shadow of shrill river growth,
So steadfast are the river's arms beneath.

Pale petals follow her in very faith,
Unmixed with pleasure or regret, and both
Her maidly hands look up, in noble sloth
To take the blossoms of her scattered wreath.

No weakest ripple lives to kiss her throat,
Nor dies in meshes of untangled hair;
No movement stirs the floor of river moss.

Until some furtive glimmer gleam across
Voluptuous mouth, where even teeth are bare,
And gild the broidery of her petticoat. . . .

PARSIFAL IMITATED FROM THE FRENCH
OF
PAUL VERLAINE

CONQUERED *the flower-maidens, and the wide embrace*
Of their round proffered arms, that tempt the virgin boy;
Conquered the trickling of their babbling tongues; the coy
Back glances, and the mobile breasts of subtle grace;

Conquered the Woman Beautiful, the fatal charm
Of her hot breast, the music of her babbling tongue;
Conquered the gate of Hell, into the gate the young
Man passes, with the heavy trophy at his arm,

The holy Javelin that pierced the Heart of God.
He heals the dying king, he sits upon the throne,
King, and high priest of that great gift, the living Blood.

In robe of gold the youth adores the glorious Sign
Of the green goblet, worships the mysterious Wine.
And oh! the chime of children's voices in the dome.

A CRUCIFIX

TO ERNEST DOWSON

A gothic church. At one end of an aisle,
Against a wall where mystic sunbeams smile
Through painted windows, orange, blue, and gold,
The Christ's unutterable charm behold.
Upon the cross, adorned with gold and green,
Long fluted golden tongues of sombre sheen,
Like four flames joined in one, around the head
And by the outstretched arms, their glory spread.
The statue is of wood; of natural size;
Tinted; one almost sees before one's eyes
The last convulsion of the lingering breath.
" Behold the man ! " Robust and frail. Beneath
That breast indeed might throb the Sacred Heart.
And from the lips, so holily dispart,
The dying murmur breathes " Forgive ! Forgive ! "
O wide-stretched arms ! " I perish, let them live."
Under the torture of the thorny crown,
The loving pallor of the brow looks down
On human blindness, on the toiler's woes;
The while, to overturn Despair's repose,
And urge to Hope and Love, as Faith demands,
Bleed, bleed the feet, the broken side, the hands.
A poet, painter, Christian,—it was a friend
Of mine—his attributes most fitly blend—
Who saw this marvel, made an exquisite
Copy; and, knowing how I worshipped it,
Forgot it, in my room, by accident.
I write these verses in acknowledgment.

LE CHEVALIER MALHEUR

Grim *visor'd cavalier!*
>*Rides silently* MISCHANCE.
Stabbed is my dying heart
>*of his unpitying lance.*
My poor heart's blood leaps forth,
>*a single crimson jet.*
The hot sun licks it up
>*where petals pale are wet.*
Deep shadow seals my sight,
>*one shriek my lips has fled.*
With a wrung, sullen shudder
>*my poor heart is dead.*
The cavalier dismounts;
>*and, kneeling on the ground,*
His finger iron-mailed
>*he thrusts into the wound.*
Suddenly, at the freezing touch,
>*the iron smart,*
At once within me bursts
>*a new, a noble heart.*
Suddenly, as the steel
>*into the wound is pressed,*
A heart all beautiful
>*and young throbs in my breast.*
Trembling, incredulous
>*I sat; but ill at ease,*
As one who, in a holy trance,
>*strange visions sees.*
While the good cavalier,
>*remounted on his horse,*
Left me a parting nod
>*as he retook his course,*
And shouted to me
>*(still I hear his cries):*
"*Once only can the miracle*
>*avail.—Be wise!*"

SPLEEN

The roses every one were red,
And all the ivy leaves were black.

Sweet, do not even stir your head,
Or all of my despairs come back.

The sky is too blue, too delicate:
Too soft the air, too green the sea.

I fear—how long had I to wait!—
That you will tear yourself from me.

The shining box-leaves weary me,
The varnished holly's glistening,

The stretch of infinite country;
So, saving you, does everything.

CLAIR DE LUNE

How *like a well-kept garden is your soul,*
With bergomask and solemn minuet !
Playing upon the lute ! The dancers seem
But sad, beneath their strange habiliments.
While, in the minor key, their songs extol
The victor Love, and life's sweet blandishments,
Their looks belie the burden of their lays,
The songs that mingle with the still moon-beams.
So strange, so beautiful, the pallid rays ;
Making the birds among the branches dream,
And sob with ecstasy the slender jets,

The fountains tall that leap upon the lawns
Amid the garden gods, the marble fauns.

MON DIEU M'A DIT: ...

God has spoken: Love me,
         son, thou must; Oh see
My broken side; my heart,
         its rays refulgent shine;
My feet, insulted, stabbed,
         that Mary bathes with brine
Of bitter tears; my sad arms,
         helpless, son, for thee;

With thy sins heavy; and my hands;
         thou seest the rod;
Thou seest the nails, the sponge,
         the gall; and all my pain
Must teach thee love, amidst a world
         where flesh doth reign,
My flesh alone, my blood,
         my voice, the voice of God.

Say, have I not loved thee,
         loved thee to death,
O brother in my Father,
         in the Spirit son?
Say, as the word is written,
         is my work not done?
Thy deepest woe have I not sobbed
         with struggling breath?
Has not thy sweat of anguished nights
         from all my pores in pain
Of blood dripped, piteous friend,
         who seekest me in vain?

GREEN

Leaves *and branches, flowers and fruits are here;*
And here my heart, which throbs alone for thee.
Ah! do not wound my heart with those two dear
White hands, but take the poor gift tenderly.

I come, all covered with the dews of night
The morning breeze has pearled upon my face.
Let my fatigue, at thy feet, in thy sight,
Dream through the moments of its sweet solace.

With thy late kisses ringing, let my head
Roll in blest indolence on thy young breast;
To lull the tempest thy caresses bred,
And soothe my senses with a little rest.

FLEURS. IMITATED FROM THE FRENCH
OF
STEPHANE MALLARMÉ

THE *tawny iris—oh! the slim-necked swan;*
And, sign of exiled souls, the bay divine;
Ruddy as seraph's heel its fleckless sheen,
Blushing the brightness of a trampled dawn.

The hyacinth; the myrtle's sweet alarm;
Like to a woman's flesh, the cruel rose,
Blossom'd Herodiade of the garden close,
Fed with ferocious dew of blooddrops warm.

Thou mad'st the lilies' pallor, nigh to swoon,
Which, rolling billows of deep sighs upon,
Through the blue incense of horizons wan,
Creeps dreamily towards the weeping moon.

Praise in the censers, praise upon the gong,
Madone! from the garden of our woes:
On eves celestial throb the echo long!
Ecstatic visions! radiance of haloes!

Mother creatrice! in thy strong, just womb,
Challices nodding the not distant strife;
Great honey'd blossoms, a balsamic tomb
For weary poets blanched with starless life.

CHARLEVILLE. IMITATED FROM THE FRENCH
OF
ARTHUR RIMBAUD

TO FRANK HARRIS

THE square, with gravel paths and shabby lawns.
Correct, the trees and flowers repress their yawns.
The tradesman brings his favourite conceit,
To air it, while he stifles with the heat.

In the kiosk, the military band.
The shakos nod the time of the quadrilles.
The flaunting dandy strolls about the stand.
The notary, half unconscious of his seals.

On the green seats, small groups of grocermen,
Absorbed, their sticks scooping a little hole
Upon the path, talk market prices; then
Take up a cue: I think, upon the whole. . . .

The loutish roughs are larking on the grass.
The sentimental trooper, with a rose
Between his teeth, seeing a baby, grows
More tender, with an eye upon the nurse.

Unbuttoned, like a student, I follow
A couple of girls along the chesnut row.
They know I am following, for they turn and laugh,
Half impudent, half shy, inviting chaff.

I *do not say a word. I only stare*
At their round, fluffy necks. I follow where
The shoulders drop; I struggle to define
The subtle torso's hesitating line.

Only my rustling tread, deliberate, slow;
The rippled silence from the still leaves drips.
They think I am an idiot, they speak low;
—I feel faint kisses creeping on my lips.

SENSATION

I WALK *the alleys trampled through the wheat,*
Through whole blue summer eves, on velvet grass.
Dreaming, I feel the dampness at my feet;
The breezes bathe my naked head and pass.

I do not think a single thought, nor say
A word; but in my soul the mists upcurl
Of infinite love. I will go far away
With nature, happily, as with a girl.

A UNE MADONE. IMITATED FROM THE FRENCH OF CHARLES BAUDELAIRE

M*adone! my lady, I will build for thee*
A grotto altar of my misery.

Deep will I scoop, where darkest lies my heart,
Far from the world's cupidity apart,

A *niche, with mercy stained, and streaked with gold,*
W*here none thy statue's wonder may behold.*

T*hen, for thy head, I will fashion a tiar,*
A *filigree of verse, with many a star*

O*f crystal rhyme its heavy folds upon.*
A*nd jealousy, O mortal! my Madone,*

S*hall cut for thee a gown, of dreadful guise,*
W*hich, like a portcullis, shall veil thy thighs;*

R*ude, heavy curtain, faced with bitter fears,*
B*roidered, in place of pearls, with all my tears.*

A*nd, of my worship, shoes will I design;*
T*wo satin shoes, to case thy feet divine,*

W*hich, while their precious freight they softly hold,*
S*hall guard the imprint in a faithful mould.*

I*f I should fail to forge a silver moon,*
I *with my art, for thee to tread upon,*

T*hen will I place the writhing beast that hangs*
U*pon my heart, and tears it with his fangs,*

Where thou may'st crush his head, and smile supreme,
O majesty! all potent to redeem.

And all my thoughts, like candles, shalt thou see
Before thine altar spread, Star of the Sea!

Starring thine azure roof with points of fire.
With nought but thee to cherish and admire,

So shall my soul in plaintive fumes arise
Of incense ever to thy pitying eyes.

Last, that indeed a Mary thou may'st be,
And that my love be mixed with cruelty—

O foul voluptuousness! when I have made
Of every deadly sin a deadlier blade,

Torturer filled with pain will I draw near
The target of thy breast, and, sick with fear,

Deliberately plant them all where throbs
Thy bleeding heart, and stifling with its sobs.

FEMMES DAMNÉES

Like *moody beasts they lie along the sands;*
Look where the sky against the sea-rim clings:
Foot stretches out to foot, and groping hands
Have languors soft and bitter shudderings.

Some, smitten hearts with the long secrecies,
On velvet moss, deep in their bowers' ease,
Prattling the love of timid infancies,
Are tearing the green bark from the young trees.

Others, like sisters, slowly walk and grave;
By rocks that swarm with ghostly legions,
Where Anthony saw surging on the waves
The purple breasts of his temptations.

Some, by the light of crumbling, resinous gums,
In the still hollows of old pagan dens,
Call thee in aid to their deliriums
O Bacchus! cajoler of ancient pains.

And those whose breasts for scapulars are fain
Nurse under their long robes the cruel thong.
These, in dim woods, where huddling shadows throng,
Mix with the foam of pleasure tears of pain.

LE VOYAGE À CYTHÈRE

Bird-like, my heart was glad to soar and vault;
Fluttering among the cordages; and on
The vessel flew, under an empty vault:
An angel drunken of a radiant sun.

Tell me, what is that gray, that sombre isle?
'Tis Cythera, famed on many a poet string;
A name that has not lacked the slavering smile;
But now, you see, it is not much to sing.

Isle of soft whispers, tremours of the heart!
The splendid phantom of thy rude goddess
Floats on thy seas like breath of spikenard,
Charging men's souls with love and lusciousness.

Sweet isle of myrtles, once of open blooms:
Now only of lean lands most lean: it seems
A flinty desert bitter with shrill screams:
But one strange object on its horror looms.

Not a fair temple, foiled with coppiced trees,
Where the young priestess, mistress of the flowers,
Goes opening her gown to the cool breeze,
To still the fire, the torment that devours.

But as along the shore we skirted, near
Enough to scare the birds with our white sails,
We saw a three-limbed gibbet rising sheer,
Detached against the sky in spare details.

*Perched on their pasturage, ferocious fowl
Riddled with rage a more than putrid roast;
Each of them stabbing, like a tool, his foul
Beak in the oozing members of his host.*

*Below, a troop of jealous quadrupeds,
Looking aloft with eye and steadfast snout;
A larger beast above the others' heads,
A hangman with his porters round about.*

*The eyes, two caves; and from the rotten paunch,
Its freight, too heavy, streamed along the haunch.
Hang for these harpies' hideous delight,
Poor rag of flesh, torn of thy sex and sight!*

*Cythera's child, child of so sweet a sky!
Silent thou bearest insult—as we must—
In expiation of what faults deny
Thee even a shallow shelter in the dust.*

*Ludicrous sufferer! thy woes are mine.
There came, at seeing of thy dangling limbs,
Up to my lips, like vomiting, the streams
Of ancient miseries, of gall and brine.*

*Before thee, brother in my memory fresh!
I felt the mangling of the appetites
Of the black panthers, of the savage kites,
That were so fain to rend and pick my flesh.*

XXXVII

*The sea was sleeping. Blue and beautiful
The sky. Henceforth I saw but murk and blood.
Alas! and as it had been in a shroud,
My heart lay buried in that parable.*

*All thine isle showed me, Venus! was upthrust,
A symbol calvary where my image hung.
Give me, Lord God, to look upon that dung,
My body and my heart, without disgust.*

PRINTED BY FOLKARD
XXII DEVONSHIRE STR
EET QUEEN SQUARE WC

SPIRITUAL POEMS, CHIEFLY DONE OUT OF SEVERAL LANGUAGES.
BY JOHN GRAY.

... Come gente che pensa suo cammino,
Che va col core, e col corpo dimora ...

THE TREE OF KNOWLEDGE.

FROM what meek jewel seed
Did this tree spring?
How first beat its new life in bleak abode
Of virgin rock, strange metals for its food,
Towards its last hewn mould, the bitter rood?
First did it sprout, indeed,
A double wing.

Earth hung with its gross weight
  Its loins unto;
The tender wings, with hope in every vein,
Beat feebly upward, saying: "Is this the pain
"The Sooth spake of; to lift to God again
  "This blackness' dark estate
    "Reformed anew?

"Mine 'tis, of fruit mine own,
  "To work this deed:
"Earnest of promise absolute, these green
"Sweet wings; a million engines pulse therein.
"Yet can I leave not for a space, to lean
  "Upon a fulcrum known,
    "To know my need."

With which, the seed upthrust
  To God a scale;
Wondering at its fibre and tough growth;
Saying, the while it purposed: "For He knoweth
"My sore extremity, how I am loth
  "To cleave unto the dust
    "Which makes me hale."

Long while the scale increased
  In height and girth;

Cast many branches forth and many wings;
Wherein & under, formed & fashioned things
Had great content and speech and twitterings:
    Insect and fowl and beast
        And sons of earth.

    Stern, netherward did grope
        Each resolute root
Of the tree, making question in the deep
Of spirits, where the mighty metals sleep,
How long ere from its base the rock should leap;
    Saying: "Yet have I hope
        "Of that my fruit."

    Sprang from its topmost bough
        The hope at length,
Fearsome and fierce and passionate. The sire
Warmed his son's vitals with celestial fire,
Feeding him with sweet gum of strong desire,
    Lest be not staunch enow
        His godly strength.

    Until the gardener came
        With his white spouse,
Wounding the tree, and ravishing the son,
(Whence curses fallen and a world undone.)
                                                              For

For that rape, wrathfully a shining one
    Drave them with fearful flame
        Without their house.

    Race upon savage race,
        Rough brood on brood,
Defiled before it, whiles the tree scanned each;
Leaned leaf and branch to grapple and beseech;
Till, on a certain day, requiring speech
    Of the tree, at its base
        The whole world stood:

    "What hast thou given us
        "Thou barren tree?
"'Knowledge,' thou answerest? Thou hast set
        "agape
"The door of Knowledge only. Thy limbs ape
"Some truth. We love thee not, nor love thy
        "shape.
    "Imposture, thus and thus
        "We fashion thee."

    Sorely then handled it
        The gardener's sons.
Strangely they built it newly, having cleft
Its being all asunder; stem bereft

Of quivering limbs, save one to right and left,
    Urging the selfsame wit
        It gave them once.

    "Lo! all my glories fall.
        "Of these my woes,
"What know those wrathful men, save, in yon
        "place,
"Perhaps, yon athlete, stripped for my embrace?
"If longing cheat me not, writ in his face,
    "He knows about it all,
        "He knows, he knows.

    "Sorrow! What sin they now,
        "Those wrathful men?
"Passion! thou'rt come to me again too soon;
"Too hot thou givst me back the fiery boon
"I gave thee; love consumes me, that I swoon;
    "Thou, on my topmost bough,
        "My fruit again."

VAUQUELIN DE LA FRESNAYE.

BEAUTIFUL soul, whose heart for ever
 glows
With chaste and lofty thought thy lonely frame;
Who, living free and far from fame or blame,
Hast loved the arts, the muses, and repose;

Chastity filled, thy careful spirit knows
Earth's utmost worth; and with an other aim,
Quitting the unmasked avenues of shame,
Chooses the path where many a lily blows;

Thus unremitting, with a curious care,
To beautify thy soul with counsel sure,
And steadfast living, (treasures which endure)

Come to thy end, thou hast essayed the air,
Where thou hast found (o dove, thou white, thou
 pure!)
That counsel rare which makes the spirit fair.

❧ JACOPONE DA TODI.

❧ O LOVE, all love above,
   Why hast thou struck me so?
   All my heart, broke atwo,
   Consumed in flames of love,
Burning and flaming cannot find solace;
It cannot fly from torment, being bound;
Like wax among live coal it melts apace;
It languishes alive, no help being found;
Seeking a grace to fly a little space,
A glowing furnace is its narrow pound.
     In such a deadly swound,
     Alas, where am I brought?
     Living with death so fraught!
     O leaping flames of love!

Before I ventured forth I dared demand
The love of Christ, expecting only sweet;
Thinking in peace of sweetness I could stand
Without a pain; but, being come to it,
I suffer torments of a molten brand;
And all my heart is melted by its heat.
     I find no figure meet
     To tell this curious smart,
     To live without a heart,
     Daily to die of love.
                                   Ah!

Ah! I have lost my heart and all my sense,
Desire and all delight and all sensation;
All beauty seemeth filth to me; and hence
Pleasaunce and power of riches are damnation.
A laden tree of love for recompense,
Set in my heart, doth yield me consolation;
    Maketh great alteration;
    Doth brook no least delay;
    Thrusts out and drives away
    Sense, strength and my self-love.

To purchase this one thing I ventured all
The world; in this exchange gave all I had.
If I had all things ever made, to call
My own, I give them freely and were glad.
But love deceived me somewhat; I gave all,
And now I know not whither I am led.
    And people think me mad.
    Now that I have been bought;
    They set my worth at naught;
    I am undone by love.

My friends imagined they could call me back;
My friends who travel by another road;
The slave is helpless to forsake his track,
Nor can the bondman lay aside his load.

Sooner the stone might soften and be slack
Than love, who holds me in his strait abode.
    Oh, to my soul a goad!
    Love burns it through and through.
    Transformed, united, who
    Can sunder it from love?

Not iron nor the fire can separate
Or sunder those whom love doth so unite.
Not suffering nor death can reach the state
To which my soul is ravished. From its height,
Beneath it, lo! it sees all things create;
It dominates the range of dimmest sight.
    My soul, by what a flight
    Hast thou this high reward?
    It is of Christ the Lord;
    Embrace the Lord of love.

I have no longer eyes for forms of creatures.
I cry to him who doth alone endure.
Though earth and heaven exhaust their varied
    natures,
Through love their forms are thin & no wise sure.
When I had looked upon his splendid features,
Light of the sun itself was grown obscure.
    Cherubim, rare and pure

> By knowledge and high thought,
> The Seraphim, are naught
> To him who looks on love.

If such a love confoundeth all my wit,
Against me let no blame henceforth be held.
No heart could fly if love should beckon it.
No heart could brave the anguish I have felt.
How is it able to endure such heat?
How is it that the poor heart doth not melt?
> Ah! if I but beheld
> A soul to take a part
> Of pity for my heart,
> To know the pains thereof!

I would love more and better if I could.
My heart hath uttered all it ever knew.
I am not able, freely as I would,
To give the already given gift anew.
I gave myself, to hold, for all my good,
This Lover who reneweth bone and thew.
> Beauty antique and new,
> Since that my heart hath found
> Light without pause or bound;
> Oh, splendour of thy love!

Seeing such wealth of beauty, I am drawn

Without myself; am borne I know not where.
My heart doth yield, and, being held in pawn,
Like wax receives the seal love setteth there.
So rash a bargain never yet was drawn.
To put on Christ I strip me stark and bare.
    My heart, transformed and fair,
    For very love doth weep;
    Waves of its sweetness steep
    My heart in boundless love.

My soul transformed, almost the very Christ;
One with her God, she is almost divine;
Riches above all riches to be priced,
All that is Christ's is hers, and she is queen.
How can I still be sad, despair-enticed,
Or ask for medicines to cure my spleen?
    The fetid sweet from sin,
    With sweetness overspread;
    The old forgot and dead,
    In the new reign of love.

In Christ a goodly creature am I born.
The old stripped off, I am a new made man.
But with a knife my heart is gashed and torn,
Where flaming love, a molten metal, ran.
Wisdom and sense burnt off and wholly shorn,

Christ is my own, and beauty beyond ken.
    Flung in his arms' great span,
    The cry of love rings higher:
    Love, whom I so desire,
    Make me to die of love.

For thee, for love, I languish and I burn.
I sigh for thy embraces soon and late.
When thou art hence, I live and die; I yearn
And groan and whine in very piteous state
To find thee; and my heart, at thy return,
Fainteth with fear lest aught should separate.
    Therefore no longer wait.
    Come, love, to succour me.
    Compel me; bound to thee,
    Consume my heart with love.

I am grown dumb, discreet discourse who held.
Once I could see the light who now am blind.
Such an abyss has never been beheld.
But mute, I speak; I fly, in chains confined;
Falling I mount; I hold and am compelled;
I follow, my pursuer pants behind.
    O passion unconfined!
    My folly is complete,
    By reason of the heat,
    The fury of the stove.

CHRIST:
Virtue availeth not without control.
Control the love wherewith thou lovest me.
Do thou with virtue renovate thy soul;
Since thou desirest so to come at me.
Controlled and duly ordered, sane and whole,
I will the love which thou shalt offer me.
> How doth one prove a tree,
> If not by what it yield?
> Worth in this wise is sealed
> To all things, by a proof.

Everything which I have formed and made
Is made with number, measure and array.
Unto their end all things in rank are laid;
By order 'tis all things pass not away.
Love, more than all the rest, is held and staid
In order by its nature, in a way.
> But if the fervent ray
> Of love hath made thee mad
> And shapeless, be not glad;
> Fervour hath ruined love.

FRANCIS:
O Christ, now thou hast stolen my heart, thou
    say'st: "Set

"Set thy soul's love in order," to thy worm.
But how, transformed in thee, so deeply graced,
Can I be lord of me, or rule the storm?
As iron in the fire grows plastic paste,
As air transfixed by sun grows light and warm,
    And lose their ancient form,
    And take a new allure,
    So be my soul, grown pure,
    Clad on with thee in love.

Why hast thou brought me to a fiery place,
If thou wilt have me to be temperate?
When without measure thou didst give thy grace,
Thou didst confound all sense of size & weight.
Small thou didst fill my small heart's utmost space:
I have no scope to hold thee being great.
    If I be desperate,
    The fault is thine, not mine,
    O thou who didst define
    Conditions of our love.

Thou canst not shield thyself from love. Love
    brought
Thee captive by the road from heaven to earth.
Thou didst descend to lowness to be naught,
To roam a man rejected from thy birth;

No house nor field enhanced thy lowly lot;
Poor thou hast given riches and great worth.
    In life, in death, no dearth
    Of love hast thou declared.
    Thy heart hath flamed and flared
    With nothing else but love.

Wisdom remembered not to stint or rein
Thy love, when passion bade the whole be
    poured.
Thou wert not flesh, but love, in frame & brain;
Love made thee man to bear our sin's reward.
Thy love required the cross, the world's disdain.
Thou didst not profit thee to speak a word
    To Pilate, or the horde
    Of those who wrought thy woe;
    Yearning to take the blow
    Upon the cross of love.

Love, love, how thou hast dealt a bitter wound!
I cry for nothing now but love alone.
Love, love, to thee I am securely bound;
I can embrace none other than my own.
Love, love, so strongly hast thou wrapt me round,
My heart by love for ever overthrown,
    For love I am full prone.

> Love, but to be with thee!
> O love, in mercy be
> My death, my death of love.

Love, love, O Jesus, I have reached the port,
Love, love, O Jesus, whither thou hast led.
Love, love, 'tis thou hast given me support.
Love, love, for ever am I comforted.
Love, love, thou hast inflamed me in such sort,
The goal of love is reached, and I am dead.
> To love for ever wed,
> Love hath cemented both
> Our hearts in perfect troth
> Of everlasting love.

✲✲ This "Amor di Caritate" used to be attributed to Saint Francis of Assisi.

❈ LORD, if thou art not present, where shall I
Seek thee the absent? If thou art everywhere,
How is it that I do not see thee nigh?

Thou dwellest in a light remote and fair.
How can I reach that light, Lord? I beseech
Thee, teach my seeking, and thyself declare

Thyself the sought to me. Unless thou teach
Me, Lord, I cannot seek; nor can I find
Thee, if thou wilt not come within my reach.

Lord, let me seek, with sturdy heart and mind,
In passion of desire and longingly.
Let me desire thee, seeking thee; and find . . .

Loving thee, find thee; love thee, finding thee.

THEY say, in other days,
When Jove in Heaven, and Pluto ruled in Hell,
Man, walking in a haze,
Exceeding good, or did exceeding ill.

So, when he came to Dis,
And man must face his three infernal judges,
Having greatly done amiss,
The devils grin, and fellow fellow nudges.

They say that many a prince
Came with such load of crime upon his back,
That Tartarus would rinse
His jaws, that Hell would shudder and be black.

First Æacus would hear the tale
Against the sinner of his sin,
And for a pain condemn the pale
Ghost to the lower court, wherein

Dread Minos gave a like award,
And sent him Rhadamanthusward.

There was no pain for man that Hell could
    reach
Like this pain. Yet the devils would beseech
                                        Their

Their master, and entreat the Dreadful One
To judge as strangely as the thing was done.

Then Pluto judged; that is to say, his face was
    bare;
Whereof I may not tell if it were harsh or fair;

But this I may: a man might howl a space
Of many years who once had seen his face.

🌺 My patron came to Heaven; he touched the
    door,
And stood within the same.
The guardian greeted him, and walked before,
And called him by his name:
"Heaven waited for thy coming, sweet Saint
    John;
"Thy road lies bright before thee; pass thou on."
Humbly my patron answered him: "Nay, sir;
"I need but little space; I will not stir."
"He waits in state for thee who is thy home:
"Thou wilt not keep him waiting, brother;
    "come."
He met the Lover of the Dark Night's tryst;
Saint John was folded in the hands of Christ.
He lay upon their wounds, and wept the whole

Of longing that was in his holy soul.
Those molten hands were silent. And made
    speech:
"Weep not for us, sweet Pity, lest thou teach
"Us even greater sorrow than our own;
"The angels weep not, nor doth Heaven make
    "moan.
"'Twas we who made thee, holiest of thy kind;
"Who touched thy little eyes, & made them blind.
"Dying, the darkness of thy glorious night
"Was we about thee, covering the light.
"Pass on; his Passion cannot be denied."
And John was locked within the riven Side.
The Wound said: "Sleep, beloved, and be calm;
"I, in thy flesh, made wounds upon thee balm.
"My torrent poured for thee; thou art my son;
"I ached for this dear hour, my darling one.
"Thou wert a proper vessel for the Wine
"I gave thee to dispense, thou son of mine.
"Now would my love for ever close upon
"Thee; but thy house is greater; pass thou on."
And John was cradled in the Sacred Heart,
Than which no mansion is more glorious.
O friar of sweet counsel, where thou art,
John of the Cross, my patron, pray for us.

AURELIUS PRUDENTIUS CLEMENS.
HYMN BEFORE SLEEP.

FATHER, whom none hath ever seen;
And Christ, the Father's Voice, be nigh;
Kind Spirit, who hath ever been.

One force, one light, of Trinity:
God; and eternal God of God;
God out of both eternally.

Labour of day hath ceased to plod;
The hour of rest returns; and sleep,
Loosing the limbs, doth lie abroad.

When anxious, careful minds drink deep
The vintage of oblivion,
Lethe doth through the members creep;

Till not a grief doth sit upon
The mind; nor sense of wasting care
Remaineth to the woe-begone.

God's law of mercy everywhere
To fragile bodies; that a sweet
Should temper labour with repair.

Whilst

Whilst rest through all the veins doth fleet,
And soothe the breast with whelming sleep,
Wherein the quiet heart doth beat,

With strong-winged strength the sense doth
    sweep
The air; and sees in varied guise
The things which else are over-deep.

For, freed from sorrow or surprise,
The mind, whose origin is heaven,
Inert, its source, the air, denies.

Through all its native phases driven,
It loves the thousand flights unflown,
Joys in the subtle action given.

The sense of those in slumber prone
The unlearnt splendour wanders through
Which gives the future to be known.

But lying images (the true
Being hence) the spirits, sad with fear,
Deceive with wiles not small nor few.

Whom life with faults hath failed to smear
                                                    Too

Too frequently, the vibrant light
Teacheth, and bringeth deep things near.

But unto him whose heart, unright,
With vice hath fouled him—him, distressed,
Terror shows visions which affright.

The faithfullest evangelist
Of Christ saw in the distant cloud
Hid signs, and hidden knowledge wist:

The Lamb of God, in purple shroud
Of slaughter, who unsealed the book,
(None else with grace enough endowed)

Whose great hand, armed with lightning, took
The two-edged sword in his control,
And threatening a double stroke.

Sole judge of body this, of soul,
And this sword, doubly to be shunned,
Is the two deaths, the double dole.

John, the just hero, thus unbound
His mind with sleep that, with his ghost,
Free it might tread ethereal ground.

Dó not let us increase the host
Of those whom thronging errors fill,
Whose vain desires are uppermost.

Enough for us if sweet and still
Repose refresh the wearied frame;
If sleep portend us nothing ill.

Remember, bearer of Christ's name,
The sacred dew of baptism, dread
Lest thou shouldst bring it into shame.

Sleep calling, finding thy chaste bed,
See that the figure of the cross
Be signed upon thy breast, thy head.

All sin and darkness fly the cross,
And, designated with such sign,
The mind to swerve is at a loss.

May no grim portents undermine
Our sleep, of roving dreams; be far
The Liar, with his dark design.

O tortuous serpent, thousand are
                                                                  Thy

Thy lithe meanderings of fraud,
Seeking the calm of hearts to mar.

Hence, Christ is here, go far abroad;
Hence, Christ is here; thyself hast known
This sign, which damns thy neighbourhood.

The drooping body, sunk and prone,
Is suffered to lie back a space;
Even in sleep, vouchsafed the grace
The love of Christ to think upon.

❀ SAINT AMBROSE.
❀ MORNING HYMN.

❀ SPLENDOUR of the Father's glow,
Light proclaiming out of light;
In the morning day doth show
Light renewed to bless the sight.

Beam, true sun, upon our coast,
Brightening with eternal light;
Lightening of the holy Ghost
Pour into our senses' night.

Hail with vows the Father's face,
Glorious with eternal rays;
Hail the Father's potent grace,
To repair our slippery ways;

To vouchsafe us active deeds;
Blunt the teeth against us set;
To assist our better needs;
Grace of suffering to beget;

Rule our hearts and reign therein;
(Body stern and sweet from sin)
Warm our faith with fervent heat;
Far from us remove deceit.

Faith

Faith our drink, be Christ our food,
Christ our health, our daily Host;
Joyful may we drink the good
Vintage of the holy Ghost.

Joyful is the day doth run.
Shame is morning's bursting husk.
Faith is like the noonday sun.
Mind, be wary of the dusk.

Let Aurora drive the sun,
Bland alike to man and herd.
In the Father all the Son;
All the Father in the Word.

❧ SAINT AMBROSE.
❧ SAINT JOHN THE EVANGELIST.
❧ THROUGH the love of Christ the Lord,
Called with James the thunder's son,
In his revelation, John
Knew the secrets God had stored.

He was wont by catching fish
To support his father's age;
Rocking to the salt sea's rage,
Firm in faith as faith could wish.

Dropping deep his baited hook,
John upfished the living Word;
Casting limp nets overboard,
Life for all a prey he took.

What a fish is pious faith,
Which the world's salt flood doth breast!
Resting on the sacred Breast,
Spake to John the holy Wraith:

"In the beginning was the Word,
"And the Word was nigh to God;
"And the Word was God, which was
"I' the beginning with the Lord;
                                        "Everything

"Everything by him was made."
And himself, acclaimed with praise,
By the Spirit crowned with bays,
John is crowned with what he said.

Who, by hands unholy bound,
Rudely plunged in boiling oil,
Was but cleansed of earthly soil;
Whole stood forth, with victory crowned.

SAINT AMBROSE.
HYMN OF VIRGINITY.

JESUS, virgins' shining crown,
Whom thy mother did conceive,
She a virgin and alone,
Do thou this our vow receive.

Who dost feed where lilies grow,
Set about with virgin quires,
Unto whom his grace doth flow
Whom the light of heaven attires;

Wheresoever thou dost flee,
Lo! thy virgins' tuneful crowd
Joyful follows after thee,
Singing sweetest hymns aloud.

We implore thee, more and more
Teach us in our minds to shun,
Wholly, utterly ignore,
All the mischief sin hath done.

B. NOTKER THE MONK OF ST. GALL.
FOR THE FEAST OF ST. DENIS.

LET all the brothers solemnly rejoice;
Thereunto let the whole church add its voice.
This day the glorious Dionysius,
With his companions, Eleutherius
And Rusticus, superb in martyrdom,
And crowned therewith, attained to heaven, their home.
In Athens once the saint surpassed in wit,
Where he was called the Areopagite,
Amongst his fellows reckoned first of all;
Yet spurned he, at the bidding of Saint Paul,
The summit of his power, and wisdom's pride,
And all the glory of the world beside;
By whom informed, baptised and godly grown,
He came a doctor into Athens town;
Which, radiant like one who bears a light,
He drew from darkness and from error's plight;
Gave holy dogma to his native land
And neighbouring peoples upon every hand.
This done, and being instinct with holy love,
The Apostolic mission bade him move
To distant peoples (to give true for false)
And the forbidding kingdom of the Gauls;
Declaring

Declaring unto whom the living Word,
And many men converting to the Lord,
Being rudely taken by the untoward,
With his companions, by a godless sword,
For Christ, he reached the martyrs their award.
O city Paris, o thou fortunate,
The bones to have known of martyrdom so great.
And not less happy Ratisbon, o thou
Which great authority did late endow,
Which shelterest those blessed relics now.
These and all people shield from Satan's snares;
For help commend with thy unceasing prayers
Unto the King of kings, o glorious,
O ancient martyr, Dionysius.

SAINT BERNARD.
TO THE SACRED BREAST.

HAIL, o Jesus, my salvation;
Jesus, hail, my adoration;
Hail, thou breast all passion slaking,
Only to be pressed with quaking,
    Of Love's own house the door.

Hail, thou throne of holy godhead,
Ark of charity embodied;
Peace and pause for those who plodded;
Station for the feeble-bodied;
    The bed of humble poor.

Hail, o Jesus, rich in pity;
Worthy goal of all entreaty;
Lord, reward my waiting, yearning;
Kindle me with holy burning,
    For Love's sake, heartily.

Fashion me a breast all holy,
Burning, contrite, sighing, lowly;
Disposition self-denying,
Humble faith on thee relying,
    And ever turned to thee.

Jesus, shepherd ever wary,
Son of God and holy Mary,
Let the fount of thy heart's fulness
Wash me wholly of my foulness,
    Father compassionate.

Image of the godhead, splendid
God of God, to earth descended,
From the richness of thy treasure,
Clement, fill with bounteous measure
    The poor and desolate.

Breast of Jesus Christ of sweetness,
Lo, I trust thy gift's completeness;
From my sins by favour shriven,
Flames of love have wrapt and riven
    My ever careful heart.

Thou art that abyss of knowledge;
Chorals of the angel college
Praise thee ever; John, by pressure
To thee, drank the flowing treasure
    From out the sacred Heart.

Fount of mercy, I adore thee;
Low, in love, I bow before thee;

Godhead's

Godhead's likeness in thee dwelleth;
Counsel which thou givest healeth
    In me my earthly taints.

Sanctuary of God, I greet thee;
Pity me, I do entreat thee;
Ark of goodness, vase of riches,
Let me, crowning all my wishes,
    Be numbered with thy saints.

SAINT BERNARD.
TO THE STABBED SIDE OF JESUS.

I HAIL thee, thou most holy Man.
To pardon, heal and quicken,
How didst thou suffer thrall and ban,
How was thy Body stricken!
Low all my soul in worship bows
To thee, my Saviour's Side;
Thou noble Fount, whence ever flows
His Blood to wash the sins of those
For whom their Saviour died.

Lord Jesus, see, I cling to thee,
Vouchsafe me thy salvation;
Save in thy wounded Side, for me
There rests no consolation.
O precious Wound, be thou adored,
Thou open door of grace,
Wherefrom the blood and water poured,
To pay our price from mercy's hoard,
And banish our disgrace.

My heart refreshed is like to burst,
Filled from thy savourous flagon;

         Thy

Gerhardt's version.

Thy torrent heals my aching thirst,
The poison of the dragon.
Open thy gates, thou darling Wound,
And let my heart, too bold,
Be swept away, and wholly drowned,
As in a flood which breaks its bound:
So shall I be consoled.

Craving to touch the saving flood,
My mouth looks up with yearning;
Through marrow, sinew, bone and blood,
The life-sap runneth burning.
Ah, sweet and sweeter art thou yet,
Lord Jesus, to my heart;
Who loves thee well shall well forget
The sting of death, and even sweet
Find death's own bitter smart.

Conceal me, Wound; within thy cave
Locked fast, no thing shall harm me;
There let me nestle close and safe,
There soothe my soul and warm me.
When I shall feel death's cold distress,
And when the hellish beast
Against my soul and me shall press,
Then let me, in thy faithfulness,
Quietly, Saviour, rest.

ADAM OF SAINT VICTOR.
THE HOLY EVANGELISTS.

BROTHERS, break in jubilation
To the Father of salvation;
Recollect the revelation
    Of the seer Ezechiel.
John, by sight and high permission,
Bears him out with great precision;
"Truly saw I, in a vision,
    "That which now I truly tell."

Round the throne of God, most solemn,
(Blessed ghosts in many a column)
Fourfold varied fashion feigning,
    Stand the animals of God.
First an eagle's form appeareth;
One a lion's image weareth;
Man and ox the twain remaining;
    Four are they, the beasts of God.

Fourfold forms of these four creatures
Mark the four Evangels' features,
Whose instructions heal and ease us,
    Bless the church with gentle rain.
Matthew first, and Mark the second,
Luke, and whom the Saviour beckoned,

Whom his father sent to Jesus,
 Bidding him leave nets and gain.

Matthew shape of man is given;
For he tells how God from heaven
Came, and was from man descended
 Whom himself had formed and made.
Luke a bullock's image beareth,
Forasmuch as he declareth
What the sacrifice portended,
 What its inner sense pourtrayed.

Calling through the desert places,
Mark, a lion, roars his message:
"Room for God! prepare a passage;
 "Cleanse the evil heart from sin."
John is borne to where his place is,
Fashioned in an eagle's fashion,
Sheer, on wings of strong compassion,
 Into light of purer sheen.

Brute, behold, the form of each is,
As prophetic scripture teaches;
But the meaning lies directly
 In the application.
Flight of wings and wheels' volution   Bear

Bear a spiritual solution:
Wheel untiring moves correctly,
>   Wing is contemplation.

Eke the beasts pourtray succinctly
Acts of Christ in their progression,
Each according to his fashion,
>   As thou hast already heard.
Man is he declared distinctly;
Bullock is he immolated,
Lion death hath deprecated,
>   Lastly he ascends a bird.

Paradise is dewed and tended,
Green and flower and fruit in season
Do abound and joy, by reason
>   Of the rivers' kindly care.
Streams from Christ, the fount, descended,
Run their fatal downward courses,
That the taste of living sources
>   To the faithful they may bear.

Drunk with drink from these outflowing,
Thirst of love for ever growing,
May we, from a fount more glowing,
>   Be more fully satisfied.

May their doctrine drive and urge us
From the sloughs of vice, and purge us;
Into the divinest merge us,
 Led from depths into the height.

❦ HYMN TO SAINT BERNARD.

❦ THE Queen of heaven reclined at meat,
Beside her Son, within the host.
The spikenard revealed its sweet,
Bernard was yielding up his ghost.

Sweet in the palate of the Queen
The suavity of Bernard's fruit.
Sweet in the nostrils of the Queen ❧
The holiness of Bernard's suit.

As she, to take her meat, reclined,
The fruit declared its savour well:
When Bernard's soul left earth behind,
The spikenard did yield its smell.

Sweet this recumbency of one;
Glorious, incomparable taste;

         Sweet

❧ However degraded nowaday the expression "odour of sanctity" must be read literally from the pens of holy & informed writers. See the last illness of Saint John of the Cross. Garth Wilkinson says: If the rose or the lily could be gluttonous or covetous, lewd or hating, the third generation of them would give out stenches .... the purity of

xlvi

Sweet holy Bernard's life undone,
Its holy odours deeply graced.

The bride hath come from Libanon,
To be divinely crowned upon:
So Bernard from the furnace came,
The holy Ghost's refining flame.

Lo, who is this that cometh up
Like dawning on the ocean's cup?
Lo, who doth spring from earthly plaints
To heavenly joys, to shout with saints?

She that is terrible in might,
Like armed battalions armour-dight;
He that is wonderful in grace,
Noble like Assuerus' face.

Be the soul in the body would add a thousand perfumes to the air. And the Vera Christiana Religio, para. dlxix: The odours into which the delights of love are turned in heaven are all perceived like such fragrances, sweet smells, pleasant exhalations and delightful perceptions, as prevail in gardens, shrubberies, fields, and woods, early of a morning in the spring of the year.

xlvii

Be thou before the Lord our prayers
Ascending rod of incense smoke;
Incline the Father of the stars,
O burning Shepherd, to thy folk.

TO THE BLESSED VIRGIN.
SEQUENCE.

GATE of crystal, salutation!
Foundry of the living ration,
Medicine of desolation,
    Mary, flower of earth.
Thornless blossom of salvation;
Branch, by heavenly inspiration,
Whence the almond's aspiration
    Breaks a way to birth.

Salutation, virtuous maiden!
Blessed womb with glory laden
    Fallen from above.
Thy entreaty, Queen, shall win us
Grace of God igniting in us
    Double flames of love.

Wonderful, a thing unknown;
    Lo, a maid conceiving;
God is clothed in flesh and bone;
    Marvel past believing.

Son of heaven and star of earth
    Wedding one another;

Lo, a novel bed of birth,
    Lo, a damsel mother.

As the prophet Moses lay
    In his osier basket,
Godhead lurked in human clay,
    In this virgin casket.

Open ear and brain alert
    At the godhead's message:
Traces melt and leave no hurt
    Of the godhead's passage.

Though a thousand sunrays pass
    Through a fastened casement,
Nothing ill befalls the glass,
    Wreckage or abasement;

Thus, and subtlier than the sun,
    (Pure the earthly house)
God, the Father's only Son,
    Passes through the spouse.

Thoughts flow outward, from within
    Chambers of the heart;

Strange conception without sin
    Ripens without smart.

Eyes accessible to ours,
    Keep the light which dowered;
Gay the garden bore its flowers,
    Mother undefloured.

Whiter than the lily is,
    Like the rose prolific,
Ask thy son's indulgencies,
    Virgin beatific.

Shield us from a dread award
    At his judgment seat;
Be we with thyself restored,
    Fed with angels' meat.

✿ SAINT THOMAS AQUINAS, CALL-
ED THE ANGEL OF THE SCHOOLS.
✿ THE HOLY EUCHARIST.
✿ TRUTH, I adore thee, hidden in the murk
Of symbol, wherein thou dost truly lurk.
My heart doth yield to thee without restraint;
For contemplating thee my heart doth faint.

In thee sight, taste and touch are all deceived;
Only by hearing hath my heart believed;
Whatever God's Son saith I credit, through
His word of truth; and nothing is more true.

Only his godhead hid upon the rood;
But here his manhood also doth elude;
Nathless, in both my trust and my belief,
I do entreat with the repentant thief.

I do not see thy wounds, the lance's thrust;
My God, and yet I trust in thee, I trust.
Make me believe thee ever, piously;
And ever love thee, ever trust in thee.

Memorial of the death of Christ the Lord!
True bread to men, the life which doth afford;

Afford

Afford my mind to live from thee, that it
May ever know thee to be wholly sweet.

Jesus my Lord, O pious pelican,
With thy blood cleanse me, who am all unclean,
Whereof one drop were able to make whole
The sinful world entire, of all its dole.

Jesus, whom veiled I see, without discerning,
When will that slaking be of all my yearning,
That, looking on thy glory, on thy face,
I am made happy in thy dwelling place?

🌼 B. JACOPONE. ❦
🌼 IN FOCO L'AMOR MI MISE.
🌼 LOVE setteth me a-burning,
When my new spouse had won me;
My piteous state discerning,
Had set his ring upon me:
The conqueror's prize returning,
Love's knife had all undone me,
All my heart broke with yearning.
Love setteth me a-burning.

My heart was broke asunder:
Earthward my body sprawling,
The arrow of Love's wonder
From out the crossbow falling,
Like to a shaft of thunder
Made war of peace, enthralling
My life for passion's plunder.
Love setteth me a-burning.

I die of very sweetness.
Yet be thou not astounded.
That lance of Love's completeness
So sorrowfully wounded!

                                                          Oh,

❦ Traditionally attributed to S. Francis.

Oh, broad the iron's meetness!
Not one arm's length, a hundred
Has pierced me with its fleetness.
Love setteth me a-burning.

Then were the lances scattered
The ballister was flinging;
And aye the blows which battered
Upon my shield were ringing.
What could protect me, tattered,
Before that engine sinking?
So was I wholly shattered.
Love setteth me a-burning.

Assailed with such instruction
That all my bulwarks bevelled,
Well nigh was I destruction
And shamefully dishevelled.
Still hear my sorrow's fiction:
Anew a crossbow levelled
Vouchsafed me new affliction.
Love setteth me a-burning.

Such perils did it vomit,
Great stones with metal weighted;
And every missile from it

With pounds a thousand freighted.
Plummet on awful plummet,
Hail unenumerated,
Urged with an aim consummate.
Love setteth me a-burning.

None missed, and naught defended
My breast from their unerring.
To earth I fell, distended,
No pulse within me stirring:
No longer I pretended
To meet the blows recurring;
I lay like one expended.
Love setteth me a-burning.

Not dead, but with a vernal
Surpassing joy made splendid;
Revived from my heart's kernel,
With strength and purpose blended,
I followed those eternal
Pathways which surely ended
Within the lists supernal.
Love setteth me a-burning.

Then my new forces verging,
In helm and harness sightly,

All his dominion scourging,
On Christ I warred right knightly.
Great skill against him urging,
I grappled with him tightly,
The dastard in me purging.
Love setteth me a-burning.

My wounds avenged, we plighted
Our troth of truce and leisure
For Love's sake sorely slighted;
Love lavished without measure.
To Christ at length united,
Made fit to bear its treasure,
My heart is warmed and lighted.
Love setteth me a-burning.

THE TWO SINNERS.
GODFREY.
OLIVER.
ALL the church is dark.
Godfrey comes in darkness.
Darkness cannot smother sin; contrition
Rises to his God before the lark.

Not a sough or gust;
Footsteps thud and rustle;
Godfrey barefoot, Christ would hear him coming;
Silence is not deeper in the dust.

Nearer and more near,
Where the calvary reareth
High into the dome its tree of sorrow,
Godfrey comes, and lays aside his gear.

Lowly Godfrey kneels;
One to one his heels set
Closely, looks towards the face of Jesus,
Which the darkness from his sight conceals.

Comes the timid, raw
Dawning; stiff and awful

Start

Start the members of the grisly Saviour,
Gleam the nails, the crown, which bite & gnaw.

Round the shapeless, dim
Head awakes the nimbus;
Bright and brighter throwing up the contours,
Arms and shoulders, throat and head of HIM.

GODFREY:
Salutation, Host!
Christ, avail thy costly
Sacrifice for Godfrey, soul unworthy.
Give me blessing of thy holy Ghost.

Salutation, Queen!
Lady chaste and cleanly;
Seek his feet, great Queen, with my entreaty;
Let not mine but through thy face be seen.

Do thou take my part,
Stephen, saint and martyr,
Saint of every saint and every mortal,
Eldest of the glorified who art.

Wounds, oh, be not dumb;
Holy wounds, I humbly
                                                      Beg

Beg your intercession for his favour
To my suit, be't only but a crumb.

OLIVER:
Godfrey, thou'rt abroad
Early, for a dawdler;
Thou'rt a sinful or a simple sinner
Thus betimes so to importune God.

GODFREY:
Christ of pity, hear!
Christ, thy feet are weary,
Nailed and fixed, o suffering Christ, and heavy;
Mine are heavier than I can bear.

Thine are heavy, Lord
Jesus Christ, in order
That thy sinner Godfrey may go lighter
In the peace redemption doth afford.

Mine, o Lord, are thick;
Drunk with mire and sickness;
Weight of weakness, weight and filth of travel,
Weigh them, make them more & more unquick.

Holy Saviour, lift
                                                            Godfrey

Godfrey from the shifting,
Clogging sloughs of time, and sorrow-stagnant
Pools, and let his feet for thee be swift.

OLIVER:
Jesus of the Cross!
Saviour, beauty's blossom,
Balm upon the wounds which itch and tingle,
Oil upon the floods which boil and toss;

Jesus, hear my prayer;
Fix and nail my errant
Feet upon thy cross for my advantage;
Stay them from their hurrying here and there.

Swift, from shame to shame,
Ever run they aimless;
All the wit and will they have is evil;
Much I wonder how they hither came.

GODFREY:
For thy stabbed hands' sake,
Saviour, take my aching
Hands, and make them firm & whole & lissom;
Bid the caked and drowsy palms awake.

OLIVER:
Lord, there is no thing
That my restless fingers
Have not done to thine and my dishonour.
Who shall check and guide their wandering?

GODFREY:
Lord, I see thy knees
Bleed and throb, by reason
Of thy hours and anguish in the garden;
Lord, thy wounded knees have little ease.

Worn, like thine for men,
Are my knees with penance;
Make them whole & glad with thy forgiveness,
For thy cross and passion's sake, Amen.

OLIVER:
Teach my knees to bow
To thy cross; endow me,
Lord, with all the grace of holy penance;
Make me ever love to kneel as now.

GODFREY:
Sorrow, Saviour, blears
Both thine eyes: but piercing

Looks

Looks thy love from every suffering feature;
Scarcely can I see thy face for tears.

Do thou dry mine eyes;
Do thou thaw the icy
Palsy of my heart, allay the fever
Which in every member of me lies.

OLIVER:
What my wilful sight
Sees, it sees unrightly:
I should sin against thee less, Lord Jesus,
Walked I, like the blind, in even night.

GODFREY:
Look on me forlorn;
Saviour, turn thy mournful,
Aching eyes on Godfrey, who implores thee.
Christ, I feel the bite of every thorn

Round thy blessed head
Sharp and hard and dreadful;
Christ, I feel thy torments in my shoulders;
Christ, my very heart within is dead.

Mercy infinite,   Pity,

Pity, pity, pity.
Christ, I have no words to tell my sorrow;
All my woe thou knowest, every whit.

OLIVER:
Saviour, would'st thou give
Oliver a living
Memory of all that thou endurest,
Make his stupid brain less like a sieve;

Had he sometimes pain,
Reason for complaining,
Oliver might love the holy office,
Oliver might be thy child again.

GODFREY:
Salutation, Host!
Christ, avail thy costly
Sacrifice for Godfrey, soul unworthy.
Give me blessing of thy holy Ghost.

OLIVER:
Jesus of the Cross!
Jesus, beauty's blossom,
Balm upon the wounds which itch and tingle,
Oil upon the floods which boil and toss.

REPENTANCE.
GODFREY.
OLIVER.

G. IS it his mercy or his judgment rod?
O. Repentance is an unsought gift of God.
G. Is it affliction, in his righteousness,
  Wrought upon man by God, for pardon?
O.   Yes.
G. Vain my salvation, vain the holocaust;
  If I repent not truly, I am lost.
O. If I repent, eternal life is sure;
  The promises of God always endure.
G. If in repentance I should fail a whit,
  It were as if I had not tempted it.
O. Repentance is the gift of God, to lift
  To living faith; it is a perfect gift.
G. God only is perfection. It is I
  Who must repent; or failing, I who die.
O. Himself hath known repentance; when he trod
  Our dark paths, sad, to make a way to God.
G. So, in his Passion, to make mercy whole,
  The iron entereth into his soul.
O. Hath he not borne our griefs, and with them this?
G. If we accept it not, we do amiss.

O. One way, repentance, leads to life, he saith
   Who lieth not.
G.   All others lead to death.
O. It is a grace; and faith and life are kin.
G. He saith not it shall always follow sin.
O. Then God have mercy on us, feeble men;
   And bring us to himself.
G.   Amen.
O.   Amen.

SAINT JOHN OF THE CROSS.
THE OBSCURE NIGHT OF THE SOUL.

I.

ONCE in the senses' night;
Obscure the night, with anxious passions
 burning;
(O happy hour of flight!)
Forth unobserved I crept;
For all my house lay sunk in rest, and slept.

II.

Secure in covering night,
Disguised, by secret stairways, none discerning;
(O happy hour of flight!)
Forth unobserved I crept,
For all my house lay sunk in rest, and slept.

III.

Under the night's dark wing,
In secret, seen of no one in my flight;
Nor saw I anything;
No lantern and no guide,
Save that which in my heart was all my light;

IV.

Lighting the path before me,
More surely than the brightest noonday light,
To where he waited for me,
         Whom

Whom all my love endeared;
Where no one else, save only him, appeared.
V.
O darkness, which hast guided!
O darkness, yet more lovely than the dawn!
O night, which hast united
The lover with the loved;
And changed into the lover the beloved!
VI.
Against my flowery breast,
Kept whole for him alone to lean upon,
The long night did he rest,
The while I entertained him,
And gentle swaying of the cedars fanned him.
VII.
His floating hair was fanned
By breezes falling from the tower above.
He, with his gentle hand,
Smiting my neck, bereft me
Of knowledge, so that all my senses left me.
VIII.
Fainting and all distraught;
My drooping head was resting on my love;
Senseless, resisting not,
I cast off all my cares,
Fallen among sweet lilies unawares.

SAINT TERESA OF JESUS.
TO CHRIST CRUCIFIED.

PERMIT not, Lord, the hope of heaven to urge
To turn to thee the longing of thy child;
Nor to forsake offending, terror-filled,
The pains of hell become for me a scourge.

Suffer me, Saviour, to approach the verge
Of Life, see thee alive, and nailed, reviled,
Thy body torn and bloody and defiled;
In thy death torment grant my love to merge.

Suffer me, Lord, to love thee in such wise
That though I had not heaven I love thee still,
That though I had not hell I fear thy will.

Because I love thee hold me out no prize.
Did I as greatly as I hope despair,
As I desire thee I should find thee fair.

LUIS DE LEON.
THE HOLY EUCHARIST.

IF it be bread we see, how doth it last
When eating it, it cometh to an end?
If God, how do we know it bread by taste?
Why doth it the mere look of bread pretend?

If bread, why doth the adoring creature bend?
If God, why doth it hold so small a space?
If bread, how is the contradiction kenned?
If God, made Maker eats without disgrace?

If bread, how can so small a thing solace?
If God, how is it sundered, bit from bit?
If bread, how can it yield the soul such grace?
If God, how do I see and handle it?

If bread, how came it down from heaven's
 height?
If it be God, why die I not of fright?

ALONSO DE LEDESMA.

LONGINUS, striking God, was trebly
   blind;
Blind in his body, as is plain to trace;
Blind in his soul, and of a wrathful race;
And blind by anger in his furious mind.

Come to the cross, uneasy and unkind,
Even to work an act so strange and base;
Which, though it cost a price of such disgrace,
Gave life to him, repose and calm to find.

The iron of the javelin he held
Serving for striking-steel, and Christ the stone,
The rood the tinder for the spark that flies,

He struck the flint, impelled by rage unquelled;
And drew the fire of love. From Mercy's throne
Gushed wine, to be the wonder of his eyes.

PEDRO ESPINOSA.
THE ASSUMPTION.

IN turquoise-hued & sunset-coloured cloud,
Within the wide imperial palaces,
Where many a white torch and candle is,
The sovereign pages of the Emperor crowd.

Shafts of a thousand fragrances are proud
To mix with amaranth and lilies' fees,
Assyrian gums and Indian incenses,
On carpets deeply piled and furbelowed.

Her mantle is the sun; the moon between
Her feet, the Virgin greets the imperial hall.
(So hoped for, this, the coming of the Queen.)

Before her feet the mighty seraphs fall
Whom joyous chorals of the angels praise.
Beside the holy Word she takes her place.

CRISTOBAL DE VILLARROEL.

UPON the tree of victory is hung
The harp of David, not Apollo's lyre.
Pole unto pole hath heard the great desire
Of three sad strings, and dolorously strung.

His harp being tuned to mourning, to be wrung
From seven stricken voices, lo! the quire
Is one: till listening Sea and Air and Fire
And Earth are shuddering for the which is sung.

The lamentable note hath reached to heaven.
Where none hath seen a tear, or heard a sob,
Now signs of grief are sevenfold on seven.

A virgin marked the song's quick grief & throb;
(The same which is the Mother of solace)
And with her tears she bathed her holy face.

TOBIAS AND THE ANGEL.

TOBIAS, journeying to Ecbatane,
Takes with him Azarias as he fares,
Which is an angel, serving unawares,
To guide and bring him to his house again.

Raphael walks mid-picture, sandal-shod;
Three fingers in three fingers leads the boy;
Holding sweet speech, the distance to employ;
The little curly dog sniffs out his road.

Tobias, jerkined, belted, simply cloaked,
With naked shanks, except for limp-legged
    boots
Against rough stones or harsh and prickly roots,
Bareheaded, querulous and wonderlooked.

Glorious archangel, Medicine of God,
Kind courier, peacock-plumed thy pinions be,
Sign of thine ancient immortality,
Folded for fare on mortal stone and sod.

Thy glory floats and glints twixt hair and wing;
Thou wearest man's attention on thy face;
Though somewhat else Tobias doth half trace
Therein, whiles thou art wise of trafficking.

Tobias bears his fish, and neatly slung,
Lest its scales soil, or it should leave a reek;
Raphael the gall, old Tobit's eyes being sick,
By sparrows' hospitality quick stung.

Hard to each hand, Tobias doth not see
Great Michael, armed and exquisite, alert,
The prince, the Warrior, lest any hurt;
Lest Asmodeus lurk to thwart, walks he.

And gentle Gabriel, the ambassador;
His arm a lily-stalk, with triple bloom,
And three locked lilies (tidings yet to come).
One with an angel maketh one of four.

Much sky and little earth complete arrear,
Tree-fledged and island-strawn, the Tigris, bland,
Creeps lower. (Pilgrims trudge on mountain land.)
Flower and thorn and stone are frequent near.

Hasting to speed thy marriage, thou and he,
Tobias, hardly yet at man's first scope,
Sprung of staunch kindliness and godly hope,
Brought up and nourished in captivity.

Forth

Forth from the river, come to take thy bath,
Leaped fleshly passion, eager to devour;
"Seize him," the angel said; and in that hour
Slit out his gall, his lust, his bilious wrath.

To medicine the gall at bidding turned
Of him who leadeth thee; the heart laid by;
The liver too, to purpose presently,
To fright the demon, being spoiled & burned.

Mark how Tobias, setting out for gain,
Under the angel guidance halts halfway
For greater gain; the guide resumes the way,
Wise and alone, to spare his ward the pain.

He sees in Azarias one of his tribe,
A man discreet and just, but hired for wages
To bring him into Media, to Rages;
Back to the city of Sennacherib.

Of Raphael's work, and how he handled it,
With fish's gall how he gave Tobit sight,
Purgation of the demon-haunted night,
Is written in the book which Tobit writ.

All things being done, and done exceeding well,

The guide replied to him, when said Tobias:
"Give we the half of gain to Azarias:"
"Call me not so, my name is Raphael."

There liveth no Tobias graced with power
To take angelic counsel, to uproot
Swarth lust, meek purity to substitute,
But meets the angel in the proper hour.

SAINT SEBASTIAN.
ON A PICTURE.

THE day is falling on a wicked deed.
A richer veil than sunbeams ever wove
With woof of air for colour stricken greed
Hangs sheer, where downward stacks of stairs
    recede,
Each ever mauver than its fellow mauve.

But inward, and beyond the keen of those
Who may behold this wonder if they will,
Keep ward such armies, in a hush so still,
The stair they stand on scarcely knows the throes
Of their unanimous breathing.   Thus, until

The holy hour they wait upon shall knell,
They curb the impatience of their harps, & hark;
Which being struck, day like a stricken bell
Shall shriek; & flee; & night cast down his fell;
And more than earthly night shall night be dark.

Earth is a landscape, where an orange grove
Has all the seeming of a labyrinth,
Even as orange as the heaven is mauve;
The sun is gold as heaven is hyacinth,
As glowing as a founder's open stove.

An insolent pavilion blocks the right.
Betwixt its golden curtains (fringed with gold)
Peer wicked turbaned ruffians, shrunk and old;
The grave sun smites the tent with level light,
Firing its crest and gilding every fold.

So yellow this against the slothfulness
Of one delicate vine, a purple-rain,
Whose lilac clusters, heavily drooping, stain
The tent's walls; the inquisitive tendrils press
Into the opening, and turn back again.

Yet somewhat wanting to this colour-plot;
Mauve heaven and orange earth are not enough;
A swarm of hell stands by, a lurid spot;
Their knotty limbs are fierce with scarlet stuff;
Their rank hair veils their ears, which hearken not;

Their faces are all wrathful, drawn and swarth;
Their bonnets are thrown back & feather-dressed;
Cloaks thrown aside; one, younger than the rest,
Too young for murder, hurries to and forth,
Bolts in each hand and sticking in his vest.

O sin! their wicked feet help wicked hands
To strain the tension of their stubborn bows.
             The

The captain, he who wears the reddest hose,
Impatient, armed, and legs akimbo, stands
Aiming, with one clinched eye & wrinkled nose.

Bright carnations leap
From the bloodred soil.
Petals soon shall drip
With Sebastian's spoil.
Oh, that flowers should weep.

Pale Sebastian's feet
Clutch the ground for strength;
For his blood doth beat
Through his body's length
Feverish and fleet.

Eyes reluctant turn
From the wicked crew;
Eyes with love which burn
For the ill they do,
Heavenward must turn.

Yet his human skin
Cannot choose but shrink,
Shamed because of sin,
Though upon the brink
Martyr palm to win.
lxxx

JOACHIM DU BELLAY.

IF our poor life be less than but a day
In the eternal, if the year in his round
Irrevocably chase our days away,
If all things born be perishable found;

What dream'st thou, o my soul, in prison bound?
Why with this earth's dark day art thou content,
If to fly out to other, dearer ground,
Thou hast upon thy back thy wing well penned?

There is that goal to which thy vows ascend;
There the repose for which the whole world sighs;
There love is; there all pleasures fitly blend;
There, o my soul, led to the highest skies,

Thou may'st the idea of that beauty meet
Which in this world I greet and find most sweet.

VAUQUELIN DE LA FRESNAYE.
EPIGRAM.

TELL me, who mayst thou be,
    who goest so poorly shod?
Religion. I am
    that well-known child of God.
Why is thy garment woven
    of such paltry wool?
Because I hold all riches
    poor and pitiful.
What book is that thou bearest?
    God my father's law,
Wherein his will reveals
    its mystery and awe.
And why with naked flanks?
    An unprotected breast
Becomes me who desire
    white doctrine for my vest.
Ah, kindliness,
    why dost thou halt upon that cross?
Because 'tis easier to my limbs
    than tender moss.
Unto what end
    art thou provided with those wings?
I teach mankind
    to soar away from earthly things.

Why is thy form so radiant
           with such glorious light?
I ward from saintly souls
           the blackness of the night.
Why with this bit and bridle?
           With it, in constraint
Of gentle fear, I curb
           the fervour of the saint.
And wherefore vanquished lies
           pale trampled death beneath
Thy feet?
           Because I am none else than death
           of Death.

TO SAINT JOSEPH.

STRENGTH of the Church by thy
    paternal care,
Master and pupil of the living Word,
Chaste guardian of the Mother of the Lord,
Be thou before thy Son our potent prayer.
Remembering him, shield us from every snare
That threatens children's feet; as once his ward
Be ours; and to our lisping lips afford
A pattern of sweet speech. As thou didst fare
Into an alien land, with patient feet,
Leading the holy Virgin and her Son
Beyond the reach of murderous alarms,
Lead us from mortal ill. For us entreat,
Who didst desist from toil, the course well run,
Supported by the everlasting arms.

ON THE HOLY TRINITY.

ERE aught began,
Beyond the span
Of sense, the Word
(O priceless hoard!)
Was, which God fashioned in his youth.
    O Fatherbreast,
    Wherefrom, with zest,
    The Word did bloom!
    Yet did the womb
Retain the Word in very truth.
    Of twain a fount,
    Love paramount,
    The double troth,
    Known unto both,
The ever gentle Spirit flows.
    Equal, and none
    Can make but one;
    One are the three;
    Yet what it be
That triple spirit only knows.
    The triple crown
    Hath deep renown;
    Ring without clasp,
    No sense can grasp,
It is a depth without a floor.

Is rest, is grace,
Shape, form and space;
The source, the ring,
Of everything;
A point which never moveth more.
To its abode
There is no road;
Curiously
It beareth thee
Into a desert strangely strange.
Is wide, is broad,
Unmeasured road;
The desert has
Nor time nor space,
Its way is wonderfully strange.
That desert plot
No foot hath trod;
Created wit
Ne'er came to it;
It is, and no man knoweth what.
Is there, is here,
Is far, is near,
Is deep, is high,
And none reply
Whether this thing be this or that.
Is light, is pure,

Is most obscure,
　　　Nameless, alone,
　　　It is unknown,
Free both of end and origin.
　　　It standeth dark,
　　　Is bare and stark;
　　　Reveal his face
　　　Who knows its place,
And say what fashion it is in.
　　　Become a child,
　　　Deaf, blind and mild;
　　　Be eye and thought
　　　Reduced to naught,
Self and negation driven back,
　　　Space, time resign,
　　　And every sign,
　　　No leader hath
　　　The narrow path,
So com'st thou to the desert track.
　　　O soul, abroad,
　　　Go in to God;
　　　Sink as a yes
　　　In nothingness,
Sink in unfathomable flood.
　　　I fly from thee,
　　　Thou greetest me;

Self left behind,
If I but find
Thee, o thou good of every good!

ANDREAS GRYPHIUS.

BEFORE myself I tremble, all my members quake,
When lips & nose I mark, & both the hollow caves
Of my eyes blind with waking, sorrow-laden waves
Of painful breath, my eyelids scarce in life awake.

My tongue, black with the fever brand, doth halt and shake
And stammer,—what I know not; tired my spirit raves
Towards the great Consoler; with the reek of graves
My flesh stinks; and the doctors go, and pain comes back . . . . .

My corpse is nothing more than veins and skin and bone;
To dare sit up is death, 'tis torment to be prone;
My ankles crave for someone who will carry them.

What skill me honour, art, and youth and a great name,

When this hour comes, when all is turned to
    smoke and flame,
When for one need, in spite of all, one is
    undone!

ANDREAS GRYPHIUS.

ARCH-SHEPHERD, ah! in search of
    consolation,
I stray, a sheep, redeemed by blood and death,
In the waste world; be shield against his teeth,
The wolf who runneth to my desolation.

Give not the fruit of terrible salvation
Spoil to the beast. The lion shuddereth
If thou bestead. Ward off the hell-bear's breath.
Give me a stall within thy habitation.

I know thee for my Saviour; call me now.
I follow thee; thou, thou alone canst, Thou,
Lead me to pasture-meadow, road and rest.

No stranger can protect, nor hireling keep.
Come thou thyself, and mark me for thy sheep.
Fold me where nevermore can aught molest.

FRIEDRICH SPE.
LOVESONG TO THE BRIDE-GROOM.

NEVER was morning's blushing face
    So beautifully tressed,
Nor, after winter void, the grace
    Of spring so fairly dressed;
The mellow breast of the white swan
    Was never yet so bleached,
Nor gilded arrows of the sun
    With brightness so enriched;

As Jesu's cheek and brow and mouth
    With grace are overflowing.
Love shoots a thousand darts from both
    His round eyes' fervent glowing.
Love has so smitten my sore breast,
    (O woe of the sweet pain!)
Love's sake will scarcely let me rest.
    I ceaselessly complain.

With tears my welling eyes are filled,
    Like bright pearls of the east;
And like rose-water twice distilled,
    My tears have never ceased.
O Eros! chastest, purest passion,

      Dipping them in this shower,
Allay thy pinions' burning fashion,
      Lest passion overpower.

Thy torch is amply sharp to kill,
    Thy wings are never idle,
Therefore shalt thou, of tears, with skill,
    Fashion thee bit and bridle;
Be not too fierce thy heat and light,
    Nor burn me all to ashes;
Be held, keep pace, and goal in sight;
    Employ thy softer flashes.

White arm of Jesus and white hands,
    The cygnet is your fellow;
Put forth the power no thing withstands;
    Be not your compass mellow;
Hold me with strength against his breast,
    Where I may make my moan
In full. I answer for the rest,
    Even were his heart of stone.

PAUL GERHARDT.
THANKSGIVING FOR BODILY HEALTH.

LET us, who are sound and strong,
Lift our joyful faces;
Open mouth and cleanly tongue,
Greet our God with praises.
Hourly to him let us raise
(All our health from God is)
Healthy anthems all our days,
For our wholesome bodies.

Sweet and sound and tender blood
Leads a bright existence;
God, in giving us this good,
Gives us a subsistence
Ample for this passing world;
For the things of wonder,
Golden tent of heaven unfurled,
Wait us in the yonder.

Were I rich as Crœsus was,
Gold and gold to squander;
Had I fame and made I laws,
Just like Alexander;
Sickly, were I forced to lie,

Beds and pillows pressing,
Would my wealth and grandeur be
Such a perfect blessing?

Were my table, passing wish,
Heaped with joy and pleasure,
Had I venison, wine and fish,
All the garden's treasure,
Which rejoices brain and heart,
Tongue and throat and palate,
What if I must sit apart
Not so much as smell it?

Had I pomp and every dower,
Sat in highest places,
Had I power of every power,
Lord of all the graces;
But suppose my body bore
Yoke and secret anguish
Of some sickness, like a poor
Beggar I should languish.

If I choose a piece of bread,
Where's the man will blame me?
Rather than the red-gold red
Filth men sigh for: Hey-me!

If my meat and drink taste well
All within my reach is;
Better cabbage to my fill
Than a dish of peaches.

Velvet, purple, help me not
Misery to carry,
If rheumatic, stone and gout,
Epilepsy harry;
Rather would I joyful go,
Ragged in meagre stitches,
Than with pain rock to and fro,
Clad in satin breeches.

Haply were I dumb from birth,
Were I lame on crutches,
If I could not see the earth,
(Light of day so much is)
Lacked I hearing, or had I
Soundless life before me,
Rather had I then that my
Mother never bore me.

Lacked I wit, or taste, or smell,
Were I muddle-headed,
If in muddle too, as well,

Heart and soul were wedded;
Were my courage and my thought
Never quite contented,
Better for me were I brought
Whence I was invented.

There is nothing wrong with me
In the parts I mention;
I enjoy the light, and see
All God's kind intention;
When my eyesight looketh round,
And my hearing heareth,
How the little birds' sweet sound
Praiseth whom it feareth!

Heart and spirit, hands and feet,
Have their proper forces;
All my fortune floweth fleet;
And I run my courses,
Which my master hath ordained
For my little sojourn,
Till the guerdon I have gained
Those who briskly budge earn.

While I draw the breath, with joy,
Which thy bounty giveth,

Let my body well employ
Gifts which it receiveth.
May my members, soon and late,
Both in sleep and waking,
Ever to thee dedicate
Every undertaking.

Hold me by thy power and strength,
When I feel death's finger,
And my little hour, at length,
Warns me not to linger.
Give me quietly my time,
With no grave affliction,
And in heaven thy sublime
Joys beyond prediction.

❀ THE TWELVE PRECIOUS STONES.
❀ THE ABBESS HERRAD VON LANDSPERG. ❀

❀ CHILDREN of the heavenly land,
In a chorus praise your band
Him, the King of kings, who planned
Heaven's structure, him whose hand
Built his house, by whose command
Its foundations ever stand.

JASPER, with its virid hue,
Shows the counsel of the true;
Which, with virtues not a few,
Never inwardly doth fade;
At whose company arrayed
Satan turns and is dismayed.

SAPPHIRE hath the look alone
Of the blue celestial throne:

Images
❀ Herrad was Abbess of Hohenburg in Alsace at her death in MCXCV. According to the record she was admirable in her office. Her celebrated MS., the "Hortus Deliciarum," and the only copy of it, was destroyed by the Prussians in MDCCCLXX. There seems no call to defend
xcix

Images the hearts of those
Who in hope are simple; whose
Life correct and conduct even
Do delight the King of Heaven.

CHALCEDONY doth aspire,
In its seeming, unto fire.
First it swirls in smoky froth,
Then in lightning darteth forth:
Means the faith of those who serve
Secretly and never swerve.

EMERALD, exceeding green,
Doth present an olive sheen.
This is faith of all most deep,
Which for good doth ever keep
Open heart, and never tires
Of good works and good desires.

※ ※ ※ ※ ※ ※ ※ ※ ※ ※ ※ ※ ※

her theology, and a quotation from the poem here
translated shall speak for her Latin poetry:

Sardius est puniceus,
Cujus color sanguineus,
 Decus ostendat martyrum
 Rite agonizantium;
Sextus est in catalogo,
Crucis hæret mysterio.

c

SARDONYX is tricolor,
Shows the man interior;
Humbleness from black grown white;
Chastity of whitest light;
Crowning all the goodly sum,
Glows the rose of martyrdom.

SARDIUS is purple red,
Like the blood of those who bled,
Glorious martyrs of the faith,
For their honour done to death.
Precious Sard is number six,
Mystery of the crucifix.

CHRYSOLITE, for goldness, doth
Sparkle like an oven's mouth;
Therefore shows the wont of men
Who are wise beyond our ken;
Wearing graces sevenfold,
Shine with them as 'twere with gold.

BERYL is a liquid gem;
Bright and pure as when a beam
Cleaveth water. This reveals
Longing of the heart which feels
That the calm of mystic rest
Is the highest, blessed best.

TOPAZ is a stone most rare,
Costlier than others are;
Gloweth with a golden sheen;
Hath a most ethereal mien;
In its contemplativeness
Means life's serious business.

CHRYSOPRASE doth imitate
Purple stuffs of royal state.
Stained with drops like golden dew
All its purple body through,
Perfect charity doth show,
No rebuff can overthrow.

HYACINTH, as to its hue,
Is of mediocre blue.
Notably, its beauteous face
Changeth with the time and place.
Signifies angelic sense
Perfect in obedience.

AMETHYST a place is set
For its lovely violet.
Throwing out its golden flames
And its purple sparks, proclaims
Hearts of humble men despised,
Who, by faith, are dead with Christ.

These

These are all the precious stones;
Types of men in flesh and bones.
Varied colour, varied tone,
Every virtue in its zone;
Flowering with these a man
May become a citizen.

O JERUSALEM of peace,
All thy roots are laid in these.
Nigh to God and happy be
All the souls which merit thee.
And the guardian of thy towers
Never sleeps nor wane his powers.

MADAME GUYON.

AND if to love be counted shame,
Then those who choose to blame, must blame
The Lord himself, who claims my love.
>   This hour forth I swear
>   Him alone to love,
>   Always, everywhere.

I do not understand at all
How they suppose a narrow cell
Can hinder me from loving him.
>   Can a prison fence
>   From the power supreme,
>   Baulk omnipotence?

Could I forbid myself to love
Who charmeth all, below, above,
Him who is love's true counterfeit?
>   Wonderful command,
>   Kindness infinite,
>   Who can understand?

If it were but a privilege,
My soul would dare itself the pledge
That thou wouldst suffer its desire.
>   But thine own command,

    In my heart a fire,
    None shall countermand.

I am indifferent to the smart
With which they would afflict my heart,
Seeking the brand of love to cool.
    But they do not know
    God doth hold my soul
    Where his flagons flow.

Be all my heart a smart, for I
Would die if there were need to die;
The chance would be too great to miss;
    Glorious at my fate,
    Leaving all for his
    Love immaculate.

The while they struggle with my love,
They do so, thinking they can move,
And cast love from his stalwart throne.
    But their ruffian hands
    Strengthen it alone,
    Closer knit the bands.

When thou didst speak thy Law in thunder,
Worthy object of our wonder,

Mystery known to thee alone,
    Thy almighty hand
    Wrote not on the stone
    That divine command.

Thy servant Moses says the law
Is law unto man's heart for awe;
Only the heart doth understand;
    There thou writest it;
    As the heart is bland
    Deeply is it writ.

Who, loving God, loves aught beside,
Doth love amiss; love is denied
Whilst love remains to love him more.
    Those whose niggard love
    Yields not all its store
    Do not love enough.

Who loves for gain, no matter what,
Derides the law and loves him not;
The Law says: Love with all thy might;
    Bowing down thy soul,
    Body, heart and sprite.
    Be thy passion whole.

God to adore because of fear,
Or to enjoy his favour here,
Is that not loving him for gain?
    What a fashion of
    Paying back again
    God, who died of love!

Then love him without littleness
Who loveth us to such excess,
With love so bounteous and so pure,
    Lord, thy law's decrees
    Happiness insure,
    Choke my heart with peace.

Against the soul what prison serves
Whose freedom God himself preserves?
To whom it flies, a trusting bird;
    Nestles in his hands;
    Lacking power or word,
    Laughs at mortal bands.

His hands repair my weariness,
And wipe away my eyes' distress.
There laden looks of tenderness
    Whisper me the vow,
    Give me the caress,
    Which his lovers know.

My Lord came to me yestereve,
Saying: My darling, do not grieve;
Who sets a boundary to my power?
    Soon, with staunched desire,
    Comes to thee an hour
    Flaming with my fire.

MADAME GUYON.
SPIRITUAL DEPICTED IN NATURAL CHILDHOOD.

Si je commence une chanson
Je prends toujours le même ton.

THE child knows nothing of similitude.
No thought of virtue enters in his head.
He cares not whether he go frocked or nude.
He knows not if he be alive or dead.

For merest trifles he will break his heart.
He loves the shallow rather than the deep.
That which he holds is sacred and apart.
In one same moment he can laugh and weep.

He only sees what serves his present prank.
He does not reckon day nor time nor place,
Nor parents, friends, nor value, fashion, rank;
Even that he knows not God is no disgrace.

Feeble and small, he lives without the sense
Of haunting shame; to honour he is blind;
And all his wisdom is his innocence.
His smallest gesture shows his inmost mind.

Over and above he looks for a caress;

And, if the smile he covets be withheld,
His little tears, his miniature distress,
The hardest heart to instant pity melt.

cx

PAUL VERLAINE.
THE lamb seeks bitter heath to eat;
The salt it is he loves and not the sweet;
Like falling rain upon the dust his rustling feet.

To reach his end, by nothing stayed,
He butts and thrusts with great strokes of his
 head;
Then, clamouring for his dam, is anxiously
 obeyed.

God's Lamb, thou Saviour of us men;
God's Lamb, who tell'st us passing to our pen;
God's Lamb, have pity of us that we are but
 men.

Give us thy peace; o Lamb, abate
For us the terror of thy dread just hate;
O God, the only son of God the Uncreate.

EPIGRAM.

WHEN Oliver was twenty-eight years old,
Spirit and soul made speech, and this was told:
SPIRIT. I came from a grey city, patched with
    green;
The largest city earth has ever seen.
SOUL. Great space and many cities have I trod.
Memory halts, save that I came from God.
SPIRIT. I go to a cool rest and shady earth,
Where all I loved shall seem of little worth.
SOUL. I hold a pilgrimage; my feet are shod.
The light lacks forward, but I go to God.
SPIRIT. I fare a-stringing beads; I tell the span
Of certain years, which make the life of man.
SOUL. Time halts not, nor is anything effaced;
I never loiter, and I make no haste.
SPIRIT. Of all the moments I have held most
    brave,
I hold this one most critical, most grave.
SOUL. My tale is wrought of chequered shame
    and bliss;
But all my moments culminate in this.
SPIRIT. Strange, we, of various origin and tide,
In fear and aspiration coincide.
SOUL. Here, as we tenant Oliver's clay frame;
Soul, wraith and body, are we not the same?

❧ HERE ends this edition of Spiritual Poems, chiefly done out of several languages by John Gray. With frontispiece and border designed and cut on the wood by Charles Ricketts, under whose supervision the book has been printed at the Ballantyne Press.

Sold by Messrs. Hacon & Ricketts, lii Warwick Street, near Regent Street, London. mdcccxcvi.